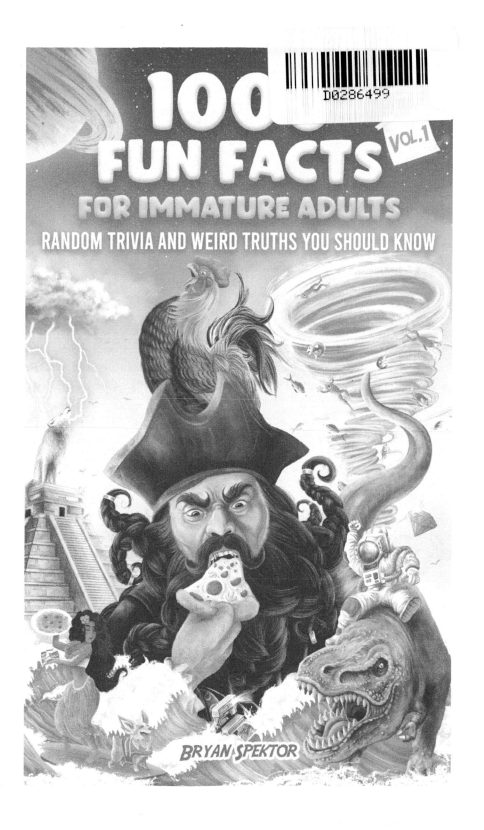

100 FUN FACTS

VOL.1

FOR IMMATURE ADULTS

RANDOM TRIVIA AND WEIRD TRUTHS YOU SHOULD KNOW

BRYAN SPEKTOR

Boring Legal Stuff to Cover My Ass...

Get it? It's a donkey, and he's in the shade. Burro na sombra.

© Copyright 2022 Bryan Spektor

1000 Fun Facts for Immature Adults

Random Trivia and Weird Truths You Should Know Vol. 1

Bryan Spektor

150 Mind-Blowing Bonus Facts

Don't Forget Your 3 FREE Books!

If *1000 Fun Facts for Immature Adults* is the approved theatrical release, then bonus chapters one and two are the unrated deleted scenes. The facts within them might be too real for general audiences and are reserved only for the most curious of cats with a few extra lives to spare. The third bonus is the post-credits scene to lighten up the mood.

Get your three FREE books when you join Bryan Spektor's spectacular, factacular newsletter at www.itsnotbs.com (no apostrophe needed). Or simply scan the QR code below for instant access:

Contents

Introduction

Do you remember when everything was mind-blowing and any little discovery felt like the biggest adventure ever? Those were the good times. Just because you're now an adult full of responsibilities, it doesn't mean the good times have to stop.

You may sometimes feel like nothing much is new or exciting anymore, but the truth is now that you're all grown up, you have way more new and exciting things to learn about than you could ever imagine.

We made this book because we want you to feel like an overly curious kid again every time you read it. We hope our little passion project reignites that sense of awe and childhood wonder within you and that it reminds you of the simple joy of discovery.

To make sure you don't drown in a sea of endless text during your journey, my wife, who we'll call Momoko, and I drew some really neat art for this book you won't find anywhere else.

1000 Fun Facts for Immature Adults Vol. 1 is packed to the gills with totally unbelievable but 100% true facts.

It's an awesome bathroom reader that will keep you on the can so long that your legs go slightly numb. It also doubles as an eye-catching coffee table book full of ice-breakers for when you have guests. And it works great as a safe-for-work gift for the next office party or secret Santa.

Reading this book probably won't make you richer or better-looking, but it will make you smarter, help you dominate trivia night, will never leave you without fascinating things to talk about, and quite possibly make you the most interesting man (or woman) in the world... second only to yours truly.

I am absolutely crazy, but I'm also crazy about facts. I've been ravenous for weird and little-known trivia since before I could read. Now that I'm an adult who can both read and write —though, that's debatable— I'm excited to share my vast treasure trove of knowledge nuggets with you.

The wife and I worked really hard on this passion project of ours, pouring whatever small bit of free time we had into it between work, and family, and keeping our marriage afloat during one of the most trying times in recent history.

We're happy to report that we haven't killed each other in the process of creating *1000 Fun Facts for Immature Adults Vol. 1*. But if you don't hear from me again with Vol. 2, send help. Momoko's Japanese and they don't mess around. I'm joking! Jodan daiyo!

So, if you like looking at funny art, like being told something you don't know, and don't mind a bit of dry humor laced with more dad jokes, rhymes, and amazing alliterations than necessary, then hop in because you're in for a good time!

To the parents previewing this book, please keep in mind that this work is not intended for children. Don't worry, there isn't anything too intense here, but the topics may be a bit advanced for them. As always, keep a close eye on what your curious kittens get exposed to.

This cheeky little trivia book is actually for you parents, and for you, the free person unshackled by your own little ankle-biter. We made this especially for you, the immature adult who still laughs at farts, but desperately tries to hide that fact from the "real" adults.

See you on the other side... of this book, because you'll want to read it cover it to cover.

Chapter 1

Bizarre Facts About the Body and Mind

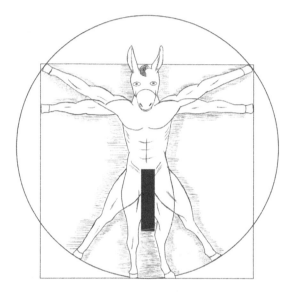

I was once that child everyone said would grow up to be a doctor someday. And I almost did, but then I dropped out of med school. Oddly enough, it wasn't the future I wanted for myself. After months of deliberation, I eventually mustered up the courage and told my dad, a doctor himself, that I wasn't going to follow the destiny he decided for me before I was even born.

Suffice to say, the feces hit the ventilation system. After things settled down, I packed my bags and went my own way. It was the most difficult but the most liberating day of my life. We made up after a while.

For children of immigrant parents, you either become a doctor or a lawyer, or you're nothing. Life was hard back home, so they struggle to understand that, in a developed country, you can find success in your unconventional passion. I always wanted to be a writer, so I did.

Make no mistake; it wasn't easy. I was met with many setbacks and faced much criticism from others and myself. In the face of doubt, all you can do is put in the work. If you have a dream but also have bills to pay, work on your dream before or after your day job, during weekends and holidays. If you put in consistent effort and put out something of value to others, you can't fail —"consistent" is the key word here.

In this chapter, you'll learn little-known facts about the amazing body you inhabit, unusual things about newborn babies, the craziest ways people have died, and the most bizarre mental conditions ever.

***

1. The average adult human body is composed of 7 octillion atoms. 7,000,000,000,000,000,000,000,000,000. That's 27 zeroes!

2. You have 4 pounds (1.8 kilograms) of bacteria in your body. The sheer number of bacteria inside you is countless times more than the entire world population. You are more bacteria cells than human cells.

3. There's enough fat in your body to make 7 bars of soap, more if you don't exercise. Yup. Soap is traditionally made with animal fat.

4. Well, actually... The adult human body isn't 70% water; it's 60%. Babies are born with about 80%, but by the end of their first year, it drops to 65%.

5. You produce enough saliva (spit) in your lifetime to fill 2 swimming pools, an estimated 25,000 quarts (23,660 liters)

6. The largest gape —of the mouth, gentlemen— is 4 inches (10 centimeters). Bigmouthed American Isaac Johnson holds the record. He can fit 4 stacked cheeseburgers into his maw.

7. Your tongue, octopus tentacles, and elephant trunks are examples of muscular hydrostats, structures made of muscle that have no attachments to bones, meaning they use muscles to move muscles. Your biceps are skeletal hydrostats.

8. Well, actually... Your tongue isn't the strongest muscle in your body. It's not even a single muscle; it's 8. The strongest muscle groups are your glutes and quads.

9. Elaine Davidson has the strongest tongue in the world. The former nurse pierced her tongue with a meat hook, then attached 250 pounds (113 kilograms) to the other end and pulled it handsfree.

10. The record for stopping the most spinning fans with one's tongue is 35. Ahrita Furman accomplished this ridiculous feat in just 60 seconds.

11. Many people assume that the ability to roll your tongue into a U-shape is entirely genetic. It isn't, but this assumption has led to much anxiety in children, who fear they're adopted because their parents can roll their tongues and they can't.

12. Every single part of your tongue can sense sweetness, saltiness, sourness, bitterness, and umami. Umami has been recognized as the fifth core taste since 2002.

13. Humans have more than 5 senses. Besides taste, smell, vision, hearing, and touch, we also have thermoception (the sense of temperature), equilibrioception (balance), and nociception (pain), and many more.

14. Umami has 3 characteristics: a full mouthfeel, a mouthwatering sensation, and a pleasant aftertaste. As the Japanese put it, umami is "the essence of deliciousness."

15. Umami is caused by glutamate, a variant of the amino acid glutamine. Examples of glutamate-rich foods are tomatoes, mushrooms, miso, and seaweed (kelp).

16. MSG is umami in its purest form. MSG (aji no moto) was invented around 1908 by Dr. Kikunae Ikeda, who first made it using kombu dashi, a kelp-based broth. Currently, MSG is manufactured by fermenting corn, sugar cane, and cassava.

17. According to the FDA and the WHO, monosodium glutamate is safe for consumption. Cooking with small amounts of MSG can reduce salt intake without sacrificing flavor.

18. Airplane food sucks because your taste buds go numb at high altitudes. It doesn't help that the food is often a couple of days old, too... *That's* the deal with airplane food, okay, Jerry?!

19. Hearing loss can dull your sense of taste. The chorda tympani is a nerve running through your ears that links your tongue to your brain's flavor processing center. People that had ear surgery report changes in taste perception.

20. You can hear and understand sound 4 times faster than your eyes can capture and process images. With a near-instant response time of 0.05 seconds, hearing is your fastest sense. You see everything 0.2 seconds after it happens... Trippy.

21. You hear music best on your left side. Each ear has a preference. The left ear loves melodies and consistent rhythms, and the right specializes in speech recognition.

22. More than 3% of the world population can't recognize the voices of familiar people. Some can't even recall their own mother's voice. People with phonagnosia can clearly understand speech but can't make out who is speaking.

23. Your ears pop when flying because air gets trapped in your body and the eustachian tubes in your ears can't equalize the pressure. Chewing gum helps the pain when on a plane.

24. The technical term for your ears popping because of high pressure is "barotrauma."

25. It's rare for your eardrums to burst at high altitudes, but at a shallow depth of 4 feet (1.2 meters) underwater, you are at risk. Scuba divers avoid "the squeeze" when descending by making chewing motions or pinching their nose and gently blowing it in a Valsalva maneuver at regular intervals to equalize in-ear pressure.

26. Because the pressure of nitrogen in the bloodstream increases the deeper they go, divers can experience a sort of drunkenness called "nitrogen narcosis." Generally, the effects of nitrogen narcosis tend to worsen after the initial 100 feet (30 meters) are cleared. Then for each additional 50 feet (15 meters) a diver descends, the effect is as if they just drank a martini on an empty stomach. This is known as "Martini's Law." Nitrogen narcosis can impair judgment and lead to disastrous decisions.

27. Resurfacing is even more dangerous. If divers ascend too quickly, the nitrogen in their bodies will form air bubbles that can blow up their joints and possibly paralyze them. They avoid decompression sickness, aka "the bends," by blowing bubbles, rising at the same speed the bubbles rise, and stopping often.

28. The average human brain can survive without oxygen for 5-10 minutes. Any longer, and there's a risk of brain death. Experienced free-divers, who don't use oxygen tanks, can hold their breath underwater for 20 minutes without injury.

29. Well, actually... You don't need to wait an hour after eating to go swimming. Your blood won't completely drain away from your muscles and into your stomach. Leg cramps can happen whether you're swimming with a full stomach or not.

30. You can get more cavities from eating saltine crackers than from candy. The starch in the crackers instantly turns into sugar, and since crackers melt and become mush in your mouth, they thoroughly stick to every nook and cranny in your teeth.

31. Chewing ice as snack will wear down your enamel and make your teeth more sensitive to cold.

32. Excluding the 4 wisdom teeth often removed in adulthood, the average human mouth houses 28 teeth. Vijay Kumar, however, possesses 37 pearly whites. He's glad to hold the world record but complains that he often bites his tongue... Fame always comes at a price.

33. In 2014, 17-year-old Indian boy Ashik Gavai had 232 teeth removed from his mouth because of a tooth-forming tumor on his jaw, known as a composite odontoma. Surgeons had to go medieval and resort to a hammer and chisel to reshape the boy's mouth.

34. By volume, the hardest substance in your body is the enamel on your teeth. Teeth aren't classified as bones because their structures are completely different. Teeth don't have a network of spongy marrow, and they can't mend themselves together and grow stronger after breaking the way your bones do.

35. Your bones are 4-5 times stronger than steel. 1 cubic inch (16.4 cubic centimeters) of bone can withstand 19,000 pounds (8,600 kilograms) of pressure.

36. The smallest bone in your body is the stapes, aka the "stirrup," in your middle ear. It's about a third of the size of a penny. The largest is the femur, your thigh bone.

37. The title for the strongest bone in the body is a toss-up between the temporal bone underneath your ears, the mandible (your lower jaw), the femur, and several others. They're "strong" in terms of how well they handle load and impact.

38. Humans are born with about 300 cartilaginous bones. That number reduces to 206 as they ossify (become bone) and fuse into larger bones in adulthood.

39. More than half of all the bones in your body are in your hands and feet. Your hands contain 27 bones each, and your feet have 26 each. 27+27+26+26=106... I promise this will be the only math you will see.

40. The first prosthetics were artificial big toes made 3,000 years ago. For whatever reason, enough Ancient Egyptians lost their big toes that there was a demand for such a device. It would be awkward to walk around in sandals without big toes.

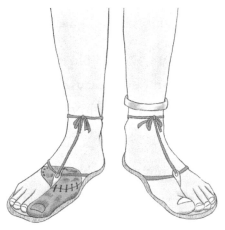

41. Your big toes bear 40% of your entire body weight.

42. The noise you make when cracking your knuckles is caused by tiny air bubbles within your joints being popped. There's no link between cracking your knuckles and arthritis, but some physicians suggest it may weaken your grip.

43. Well, actually... Nobody is double-jointed. That extra movement is due to your very much single joints having lax connective tissue (a collagen disorder), weak ligaments, or misshapen bones. Hypermobility affects 10-25% of the world population and makes people more prone to injury.

44. You don't have to be afraid of skeletons running after you in your nightmares ever again. Bones can't move by themselves. Human movement is only possible when there are muscles and tendons to pull the bones, much like puppets on strings.

45. Well, actually... None of your bones is as "dry as a bone." They're wet. Very wet. Your skeleton is 30% water, 31% if you want to be a pedantic nitpick.

46. Babies are born without kneecaps. They start out as cartilage and ossify (become bone) over time.

47. Newborn skulls compress when exiting the birth canal. Because of this, they sometimes come out looking like little coneheads. It usually resolves by itself without baby helmets or other special equipment.

48. Women do indeed glow when they're pregnant. Blood flow to the skin increases, and the oil-secreting glands become more active, leading to the pregnancy glow.

49. Some pregnant women lactate in their third-trimester when they hear other babies crying.

50. A pregnant woman's sense of smell and taste are amplified because of the hormones estrogen and human chorionic gonadotropin (HCG). This heightened sensitivity helps prevent the mother from ingesting foods safe for adult consumption but potentially harmful to the baby.

51. Well, actually... Pregnant women aren't eating for 2. The average gestating human requires only 300 extra calories to keep herself and her baby healthy. Before civilization, food was hard to come by. If our ancestors needed to procure double the usual amount of food to make babies, most of us wouldn't be here.

52. Some supportive husbands experience pregnancy symptoms like morning sickness, increased appetite, and weight gain. The condition is called "Couvade Syndrome."

53. A woman's uterus is the size of a peach before pregnancy. At peak pregnancy, it expands to the size of a watermelon.

54. The heaviest birth weight ever recorded was 22.5 pounds (10.2 kilograms). This immense infant was conceived in Aversa, Italy, by Carmelina Fedele in September 1955.

55. The biggest baby was born 28 inches (71 centimeters) large to Anna Haining Bates, a 7-foot-11 (241 centimeters) Canadian giantess. "Babe," as he was called, didn't make it past his first half-day out of the womb, unfortunately.

56. According to the National Highway Traffic Safety Administration (NHTSA), it would take direct exposure to 75 Gs to instantly kill an adult. That said, even just a few seconds unprotected in 9-G conditions can do you in by preventing your heart from pumping blood up to your brain. Astronauts endure about 3 Gs upon lift-off.

57. The highest G-force a human has ever survived was 214 Gs. During his 188th lap in the Chevy 500, race car driver Kenny Bräk crashed at 220 miles per hour (354 kilometers per hour). He sustained multiple fractures on his right femur, sternum, lumbar vertebrae (low back), and ankles. All things considered, he got off easy.

58. High voltage by itself isn't necessarily dangerous. Touching your car door on a dry day can deliver a 10,000-volt jolt, but the worst that happens is you drop an F-bomb. The real danger is current (amperage) and time. A meager 42-volt zap with a current of 0.1 amperes could be enough to make you drop dead.

59. Hanging from an electric wire probably won't shock you unless you touch the ground, grab another wire, or make contact with anything else while holding on. This is why birds usually don't get electrocuted when perching on powerlines.

60. Every year thousands of people hurt themselves trying to slice frozen bagels in half. Unlike their knives, they're not very sharp. Thawing your bagels first and using a serrated bread knife helps limit injury.

61. Avocado-hand is a surprisingly common injury. From 1998 to 2017, more than 50,400 people hurt themselves by hacking at or stabbing an avocado pit with a knife to remove it, accidentally slicing their nerves, muscles, and tendons in the process. Spoons can be used to remove the large seed.

62. It would take eating 48 teaspoons of salt to rub you out of existence. The resulting hypernatremia would make your cells shrink like raisins and cease functioning.

63. You can overdose on water. A woman died of water intoxication in 2007 after downing 1.6 gallons (6 liters) of water in under 3 hours for a radio-show challenge. It depends on your size and how fast you drink.

64. Apple seeds contain amygdalin, which turns into cyanide in your body, a deadly poison that prevents the brain and heart from getting oxygen. If you accidentally swallow an apple seed, you'll probably be fine. It's only dangerous if you crack it. A lethal dose of cyanide would require 20-40 apples' worth of seeds to be put in a blender and ground, depending on your size... Don't try it.

65. Cherries have a much higher concentration of cyanide. Just 1-3 cherry pits can put you in a pit underground.

66. It would take eating 85 chocolate bars to give yourself literal death by chocolate... Frankly, I'd be impressed by anyone who could eat that much chocolate in one sitting. Don't take that as a challenge.

67. Well, actually... Eating chocolate doesn't give you acne. Scientists gave chocolate bars to one group and some random brown bars that imitated chocolate to another. They found no significant difference in the number of zits. Acne is caused by your skin's oil glands, dead skin cells, and bacteria.

68. 1% of the world is allergic to peanuts. For some, even inhaling the dust of crushed peanuts can cause their airways to shut tight.

69. Because polio causes muscle paralysis, George W. Carver tried treating his polio patients' underactive muscles by rubbing them with peanut oil. His massages became so famous that President Franklin D. Roosevelt himself went out of his way to get a rubdown.

70. So far, there's no cure for polio, only prevention through vaccines and medication.

71. The fear of having peanut butter stuck to the roof of your mouth is called "Arachibutyrophobia." I guess that would make my dog an arachibutyrophile because he can't get enough of the stuff.

72. Consecotaleophobia is the fear of seeing, and holding, chopsticks.

73. Panphobia is not the fear of pans but the fear of everything, including pans. The fear of fear itself, though, is phobophobia.

74. That unease you may feel after learning how Surinam toads give birth could be due to trypophobia, the fear of holes or concave surfaces clustered together. Beehives, strawberries, sponges, and aerated chocolate can also be triggering.

75. Astraphobia is the intense fear of thunder and lightning. It's most common in children, but some adults never grow out of it. Author James Joyce never did.

76. Alektorophobia is the irrational fear of chickens, hens, and roosters. Tough-as-nails rugby player Tommy Seymour was terribly afraid of the domestic fowl.

77. Hippopotomonstrosesquippedaliophobia is the fear of long words... Mary Poppins' Supercalifragilisticexpialidocious must be a total nightmare for them to watch.

78. The longest word in the English language has 45 letters, and it is Pneumonoultramicroscopicsilicovolcanoconiosis. The cumbersome term refers to silicosis, a lung disease caused by long-term exposure to silica dust. Miners, masonry workers, and those in the asphalt industry are the most at risk.

79. Thanatophobia is the extreme fear of death and the process of dying.

80. There are over 200 euphemisms for death and dying. Among my favorites are "bit the dust," "brown bread," "popped their clogs," "run down the curtain and joined the Choir Invisible," "checking out the grass from underneath," and "assume room temperature." The last one is popular among morticians.

81. When you fade into oblivion, vision is the first sense to go. Hearing is the last.

82. Well, actually... Human hair and nails don't grow after death. Cadavers dry up as they decompose, which makes the skin shrink and recede... like my hairline.

83. People with Cotard's syndrome believe they're dying or are already dead —insert clever *Fist of the North Star* joke here.

84. Dr. Alice Chase, who wrote "Nutrition for Health" and a smorgasbord of other books on healthy eating, died of malnutrition.

85. More than 7,000 people die every year because of their doctor's writing. Bad writing can lead to the wrong medication and dosage being given to patients.

86. You can literally die of a broken heart. Broken heart syndrome can spontaneously occur after an emotionally traumatizing event such as a break-up or losing a loved one, leading to a heart attack in some unlucky people.

87. During his funeral ceremony in 1845, US President Andrew Jackson's pet parrot had to be removed for excessive swearing. It really must've missed its owner.

88. Brain scans of people going through break-ups closely resemble those of alcoholics and drug addicts going through withdrawal.

89. As far as your brain is concerned, getting rejected feels as if you have been physically assaulted. The same stress responses occur.

90. Acetaminophen, which is found in Tylenol, has been found to relieve the pain of rejection.

91. Erotomania is a psychological condition in which you believe a celebrity is madly in love with you.

92. The opposite of paranoia is pronoia. Those with pronoia are under the assumption that other people or unknown entities are conspiring to do good things for them.

93. The voices people with schizophrenia hear are influenced by their culture. Americans tend to hear mean and aggressive voices, and Africans and Indians hear cheery and playful ones.

94. People with the Truman Syndrome believe they are the star of their own show and that everyone is watching them.

95. Children living in abusive homes experience the same levels of fear, stress, and anxiety as soldiers during combat.

96. Knowing that something terrible will happen is less stressful than not knowing what's going to happen. Your brain likes to prepare for worst-case scenarios.

97. You're hardwired to give more importance to bad experiences than to good ones. Negativity bias dictates that for every negative experience you experience, you need five positive occurrences to start feeling lucky again. For many, optimism can be learned with enough time and practice.

98. Humans give more worth to things they put together themselves, regardless of whether it's well-built or made of quality materials. It's called the "IKEA effect."

99. People with a plan B are more likely to fail. According to the University of Pennsylvania, having options to run to when the going gets tough dramatically reduces one's ability to accomplish their goal... To be clear, this is not an invitation to burn one's bridges but to inspire one to see things through to the end.

100. Asking yourself, "will I?" is more empowering than telling yourself, "I will." Reminding yourself of your goals is more effective than making a declaration... "Will I read all of Bryan Spektor's books? Yes!

Chapter 2

Quirky Culinary Facts

Food is life. No, I'm a foodie, I'm a factie. Think about it, what are the most essential things for survival? Sleep, shelter, water, air, and? Food!!

Food is more than nutrients, though. Food is history, it's culture, and it brings people together. Your fondest memories involve food in some way. Think buffalo wings during a football game with your friends, Thanksgiving turkey with your family, and a warm apple pie made of apples you picked with gramma on a cold Autumn day.

In this chapter, you'll discover the surprising origins of some of your favorite foods, uncommon things about everyday eats, some nasty food facts that might churn your stomach, and some refreshing drink trivia. Bone apple teeth!

***

1. Before *Jurassic Park* featured the dish, the Chilean sea bass was a cheap and abundant fish. Once it got famous, its price and demand skyrocketed, and its population plummeted to the point that it almost went extinct like the dinosaurs. Chilean sea bass isn't Chilean or a bass; it's a toothfish found near Antarctica.

2. It's next to impossible to overcook mushrooms. Their cells contain chitin, giving them a very sturdy structure.

3. Be careful when picking wild mushrooms. The death cap looks and tastes just like edible mushrooms, but, as the name suggests, it can kill you.

4. Mushrooms of the genus *Laetiporus* are nicknamed the "chicken of the woods." These yellow-orange fungi taste like fried chicken and grow on trees... Don't tell the Colonel.

5. Cock ale was a popular drink in 17th and 18th century England in which a boiled rooster would be put into a vat of ale, mixed with raisins and spices, and fermented for a week. It gives a whole new meaning to the word "cocktail."

6. Well, actually... McDonald's never used "pink slime" to produce chicken nuggets. The infamous goop was beef trimmings treated with ammonia, which the golden arches used as a filler in its hamburgers until the early 2010s.

7. Let your soul rest easy; you are not a Satanist for enjoying those sinfully delicious deviled eggs. Deviled eggs have nothing to do with Satan. To "devil" a food simply means to season it thoroughly and make it spicy.

8. Until 1964, chicken wings were considered a throwaway part in America. Like other chicken bones, they were either trashed or relegated to the stockpot. Teresa Bellissimo at the Anchor Bar in Buffalo, New York, invented buffalo wings when she got chicken wings instead of necks to make stock and decided to make the best of the situation.

9. Well, actually... Boneless chicken wings aren't deboned chicken wings. They're lies. They're just chicken breasts that are shaped, sauced, and seasoned to resemble wings. They're nothing but glorified chicken nuggets!

10. Molly Schuyler set the world record in 2018 for eating the most chicken wings in 30 minutes. At just 125 pounds (57 kilograms), give or take, she put away 501 wings.

11. On Super Bowl weekend alone (just 2 days!) Americans will consume 1.25 billion chicken wings. Despite that, the Superbowl is only the second most gluttonous event in America; it's Thanksgiving.

12. The average adult will consume more than 4,500 calories on Thanksgiving Day. Most people aren't supposed to eat more than 2,000-2,500 calories in a day.

13. Well, actually... The tryptophan in turkey isn't enough to make you fall asleep. During Thanksgiving, you eat copious amounts of food, which sends your blood sugar on a rollercoaster ride. Combine that with alcohol and fatigue, and of course, your eyelids would get heavy.

14. The TV dinner was born in 1953 when the Swanson company ordered too much turkey for Thanksgiving and ended up with 260 tons of unsold product. In a stroke of genius, Swanson packaged the surplus poultry, dressed it with gravy, cranberry sauce, and other fixings into aluminum trays, then fashioned them into ready-to-eat meals. 10 million units were sold in the first year.

15. 95% of all cranberries are made into sauce, juice, and other foodstuffs. The remaining 5% are sold fresh. Raw cranberries are bitter.

16. Well, actually... Cranberries don't grow on top of knee-deep water like commercials would lead you to believe. They grow in sandy bogs on low vines. To harvest them, farmers flood the bogs, cut the floating fruit from their vines using water reels (aka "egg-beaters"), then corral them into the edges of the bog. From there a machine sucks them up through one tube and then propels them through another tube that feeds into a truck. This is known as "wet harvesting." Cranberries can also be dry harvested using a lawn mower-like picking machine. Dry harvested cranberries are the ones sold fresh.

17. Cranberries got their name because European settlers thought the fruits' flowers looked like cranes. In the Algonquin language, they're called "sassamanash." "Pass the sassamanash sauce." Say that five times fast.

18. You can test the ripeness of a cranberry can by throwing it on the ground and seeing if it bounces. Cranberries are actually called "bounce berries" in some circles.

19. When you cut an onion and cry out in pain, so does your onion. When sliced or pierced, onions release a sulfur-containing chemical called "allicin" to deter hungry predators (like us). As a reaction to the onion's act of self-defense, our eyes tear up to flush out the allicin. Garlic also emits allicin when cut or crushed.

20. According to the National Onion Association, the best way to keep yourself from crying when chopping onions is to chill them for 30 minutes beforehand. Leaving the root uncut also helps because that is where the tear-jerking compounds are concentrated.

21. Muslims are forbidden from entering mosques if they ate garlic or onions prior. It's said to offend the angels and the sons of Adam (aka other people).

22. In some Buddhist sects, eating garlic is discouraged because it inflames libido... Surely, this must be why Japan (a Buddhist country) has such a low birth rate. Surely. On a side note, Japan sells more adult diapers than baby diapers. Crazy.

23. There's a restaurant in Stockholm, Sweden, that offers an all-garlic menu. At Garlic and Shots, every item features the smelly herb in some form or another. You will find garlic cocktails, garlic cheesecake, and garlic-flavored ice cream, just to name a few.

24. The word "salad" originates from "sal," the Latin word for salt. Salata was first enjoyed in ancient Rome, where they would salt or brine their vegetables. Salata eventually reached the French. The French, being the contrarians that they are, decided to call the salted greens "salade." Then we got lazy and dropped the "e."

25. Well, actually... Caesar salad has nothing to do with Julius Caesar. It was invented in Tijuana, Mexico, in 1924 by a restaurateur named Caesar Cardini who needed a creative way to repurpose leftovers.

26. Salt was once such a valuable commodity that it could be used to pay Roman soldiers for their hard work. "Salary" and the expression "worth his salt" come from Rome.

27. The most expensive salt in the world is Amethyst Bamboo 9x. Just 1 pound (454 grams) of AB9x will run you $400. This premium salt is roasted and smoked 9 times in a flaming hot bamboo pole at 1,400°F (760°C).

28. No matter where you go in North America, you can't hide from sugar. Even iodized table salt has it. Dextrose, a sugar, is added to preserve the potassium iodide, which contains iodine. Iodine is needed to prevent goiter, a potentially dangerous lump on your neck that can affect breathing.

29. Himalayan pink salt does come from the Himalayas, but not from the Nepalese Himalayas where Mt. Everest is located. Specifically, it comes from the Pakistani part of the Himalayas, the Khewra Salt Mines in Punjab.

30. Well, actually... The difference in sodium content between pink salt, table salt, and sea salt is negligible. When pink salt is ground, its grains are similar in size to regular salt, so you're still sprinkling a similar amount. Also, there are no proven health benefits to pink salt's various trace minerals. "Trace" is science-talk for "there's barely any there." Well, at least it's pretty.

31. If you were to eat nothing but instant noodles, you could feed yourself for a whole year with just $150. The medical bills would offset the savings, though. Instant ramen is loaded with sodium, and it's linked to diabetes and heart disease.

32. 1 packet contains 165 feet (50 meters) of instant noodles, enough to cover the length of 2 basketball courts.

33. According to the World Instant Noodles Association, 106.4 billion packets of instant noodles are consumed annually. South Koreans eat the most instant ramyeon per capita, 75 packages yearly. In terms of sheer volume, though, China and Hongkong take first place with at least 41.5 billion packs a year.

34. Instant ramen was invented by Momofuku Ando in 1958 to give post-war Japanese people a quick and easy meal. The first flavor was chicken.

35. Before it was mass-produced, instant ramen was considered a luxury food in Japan. It was cheaper to buy fresh udon noodles, and healthier, too.

36. One of David Chang's favorite snacks is instant noodles. The owner of the Momofuku noodle bar franchise likes to sprinkle the flavor packet over an uncooked noodle brick and bite into it. It's a common snack in developing countries, except they crush the dry noodles in the bag, shake them with the seasoning, and eat them like chips.

37. This or that? Bloody Mary versus Bloody Caesar. The Bloody Mary uses plain tomato juice, and the Bloody Caesar uses clamato, a blend of tomato juice and clam juice, which is a briny broth extracted from steamed clams. The Bloody Caesar is basically the Canadian version of the Bloody Mary.

38. Per the FDA's strict regulations, up to 4 maggots and 20 fly eggs are permitted per every 14 ounces (415 milliliters) of tomato juice. Cheers!

39. Botanically speaking, tomatoes are fruits. They're the fleshy ovaries of flowering plants that contain seeds inside. Olives, cucumbers, and eggplants are fruits, too, though I would never put them in a fruit salad.

40. Tomatoes aren't native to Italy. Tomatoes were first introduced to Europe by Spanish conquistadors (and possibly Christopher Columbus) after they appropriated the red fruit from the Aztecs.

41. The Nahuatl-Aztec word for tomato is "tomatl," which roughly translates to "plump thing with a belly button."

42. Much of Italy's pre-tomato cuisine revolved around bread, pasta, polenta, and herb pastes. Flatbreads (the ancestors of pizzas) were topped with meats, cheeses, and vegetables. Also, lasagnas were traditionally made with beets.

43. Tomatoes were once called "poison apples" because aristocrats in the 18th century were dropping like flies after eating them. The tomato was proven innocent after people realized it was the plates they used to eat with that were the real culprits. The pewter used to make the plates reacted with the acid in the tomatoes, and that led to lead poisoning.

44. Because of the "poison apples" myth, ketchup didn't contain tomatoes until the 19th century. The first tomato ketchup was made in Philadelphia in 1812. Tomatoes were hard to come by, so factories would use coal tar, a cancer-causing poison, to increase its shelf life.

45. La Tomatina is an annual festival in Buñol, Spain, in which the whole town throws tomatoes at each other. It's recommended that participants wear white clothes. An estimated 150,000 tomatoes are tossed every year in this messy event.

46. Tapas is the Spanish version of Chinese dim sum. Tapas, which means "lids" in Spanish, involves ordering several small dishes of food to share with your table. They're called "lids" because, in the old days, patrons would cover their wine glasses with slices of cured meats and cheeses to keep bugs from getting in. Tapas used to be served for free all over Spain as complements to the libations, but now you would be lucky to still find them in Andalucia and some parts of Madrid. If you're ever at a tapas bar and don't know what to order, a safe bet would be patatas bravas (spicy potatoes), gambas al ajillo (garlic shrimp/prawn), chorizo (smoked sausage), and olives.

47. Pharmacists John Lea and William Perris invented Worcestershire sauce in the late 1930s in an attempt to replicate a sauce that an acquaintance fell in love with during his travels in India but couldn't find in England. The first batch was such a big stinking failure that they locked it away in a cellar. By chance, they opened the container years later and discovered that a wonderful aroma had developed.

48. Worcestershire Sauce, more easily pronounced "woos-teh-shuh" sauce, is made by fermenting anchovies with garlic, molasses, vinegar, and spices in a vat.

49. Well, actually... Ketchup wasn't invented in China, but it was inspired by a Chinese fish sauce called "ke-chiap." The British discovered ke-chiap during their travels to the orient and liked it so much that they tried to make it at home... See, not *all* British cuisine is bad.

50. In the 1830s, ketchup was packed into pills and used as a cure-all for the flu and other diseases. It was mostly bogus, but it's said to have worked wonders as a laxative.

51. By the time the "57 Varieties" slogan was imprinted on Heinz Ketchup bottles, the condiment corporation was already making and selling more than 60 different products. The number 57 is just there because it has a nice ring to it.

52. Ketchup flows at 0.03 miles per hour (0.5 kilometers per hour), quite literally at a snail's pace.

53. Two of Canada's most unique dishes are ketchup chips and ketchup cake. It looks like red velvet but tastes nothing like it.

54. The most expensive pizza in the world costs $70,000, and it's typically reserved for billionaires. The crust of this absurdity is lined with a whole ounce (28 grams) of gold leaf, then sauced with a 10-year-old parmesan bechamel, topped with Japanese wagyu beef that was marinated in $10,000 grape juice, flourished with foie gras flambéed in a $6,000 apple juice, stacked with slices of white truffles, covered with $16,000 of caviar, and then finally, finished with another generous sprinkling of gold... I'll take a pepperoni pizza over that ostentatious mess anytime.

55. Here are some weird pizzas from around the world: Russians eat a cold pizza topped with mackerel, sardines, and raw onions. In Brazil, their pizzas are garnished with green peas, and sometimes eggs, beats, and raisins. In Sweden, they top their pizzas with bananas and curry powder. In Missouri, it's cicadas. Yup. The bug.

56. The technical term for pizza crust is "cornicione." It means "end crust" in Italian.

57. According to the American Pizza Community, 12.5 million pizzas are sold on Super Bowl Sunday. It's also the single day of the year when the most slices are sold and the most accidents involving pizza delivery drivers happen.

58. Well, actually... Hawaiian pizza isn't Hawaiian. It was created by a Greek pizza maker living in Canada in 1962 by the name of Sam Panopulos. The "Hawaiian" part comes from the can of pineapples that Panopoulos used.

59. If you cut a pineapple in half and place the top half in soil with the crown sticking out, it will grow a new pineapple in three years. Each plant makes one whole pineapple fruit.

60. You can make pineapples flower by blowing smoke on them. Smoke has ethylene, the same naturally occurring gas that fruits release to make themselves ripe.

61. Pineapple farmers often don't have fingerprints. Bromelain, the digestive enzyme in pineapples, breaks down protein-based tissue. That's the reason pineapple rings are put on roast pork, to tenderize the meat, not just to look pretty.

62. The pineapple got its name because when it was first discovered by Europeans, they thought the spiky fruit looked like a pinecone and had an apple's sweet, juicy flesh. In many non-English languages, pineapples are called "ananas."

63. Well, actually... Pineapples aren't native to Hawaii. They're originally from an area in South America between Brazil and Paraguay.

64. The Piña Colada was invented by a Puerto Rican pirate in the early 1800s. To keep his crew in good spirits, Roberto Cofresí would make them a cocktail of rum, pineapple juice, and coconut milk.

65. Many contest its creator, but the modern Piña Colada was most likely invented in 1954 by Ramon "Monchito" Marrero, who worked at the Beachcomber Bar in the Caribe Hilton Hotel. After three months of painstaking work, he finally succeeded in making a delicious drink that captured the spirit of San Juan and soon became the national drink of Puerto Rico. BTW, "Piña colada" means "strained pineapple."

66. There's no text in the Bible stating the forbidden fruit was an apple. "Malum" means both "evil" and "apple" in Latin, so that might be how the connection was made.

67. David Rush holds the Guinness World Record for most bites taken in 1 minute while juggling 3 apples. He took 164 bites.

68. Well, actually... Apple pie is not "as America apple pie." The sour crabapple is the only apple native to North America. Culinary apples came from Asia and were brought to the US by Europeans. The first apple-filled pies were made in England in the 14th century, and the Dutch invented the lattice crust in the 16th.

69. Pies weren't always edible. In 12th century England, they were a way to preserve food by encasing it. These coffyn pastries were made of fat, flour, and water and then fashioned into boxes to be cracked open at a later time. As the world modernized, the hard coffyns gradually became soft, flaky pastries.

70. The FDA permits 4 rat hairs and 5 whole bugs per 3.5 ounces (100 grams) of apple butter.

71. Though they're used like butter on toast and veggies in a salad, avocados are fruits and berries with a single large and smooth seed.

72. Avocados are called "alligator pears" in Jamaica and some parts of Florida. This is because the fruit's bumpy skin resembles a gator's hide.

73. Avocados have names like Hass, Reed, and Bacon because they're patented strains. Their creators were Rudolph Hass, James Reed, and James Bacon.

74. Well, actually... Planting an avocado seed won't give you a new avocado tree. Avocados don't grow true to seed the way peaches do. If you plant a peach seed, it will grow peaches that taste like the original. Your chance of success with a Hass avocado seed, for example, is only 1 in 10,000. The other 9,999 will taste terrible.

75. All Hass avocados in the world come from the same tree in California that Rudolph Hass planted in the 1920s. It didn't bear fruit initially, so he considered cutting it down, but luckily for all of us, his children later discovered that the abandoned avocado tree produced delicious fruit. Hearing the good news, Mr. Hass gave it another shot. He grafted a piece of the mother tree onto younger ones. and went on to produce the most popular avocado in the world.

76. According to the California Avocado Commission, Americans will buy 12 million pounds (5.4 tonnes) of avocados to make guacamole during Super Bowl week.

77. The first-ever guacamole recipe in English was penned by a pirate, William Dampier, who wrote it in his work *A New Voyage Round the World*, during the 17th century. You could say that he's history's first food blogger.

78. William Dampier also wrote the first mango chutney recipe in English and was responsible for bringing the words "kumquat," "tortilla," "soy sauce," and "chopsticks" into the English culinary lexicon.

79. Don't get mad at your waiter if you order a tortilla at a Spanish restaurant and they don't give you a soft flatbread. In Spain, a "tortilla" is an omelet.

80. Well, actually... Peanuts aren't nuts; they're legumes that grow in pods, just like green beans and peas. Peanuts are sometimes called "goobers."

81. It takes an average of 540 goobers to make a 12-ounce (340-gram) jar of peanut butter.

82. The FDA allows up to 30 bug parts (heads, legs, wings, etc) per every 3.5 ounces (or 100 grams) of peanut butter for it to be considered safe for consumption... It makes me wonder if it's really the peanuts that make crunchy peanut butter so crunchy. That is why I'm team smooth. Less bugs... I hope.

83. The FDA is quite lax with jams and jellies. If 30% of the contents in a jar of cherry jelly are moldy, it passes. In black currant jam, it's a stomach-churning 75%.

84. The average American will eat 3,000 peanut butter and jelly sandwiches in their lifetime... That's a lot of bugs.

85. Well, actually... Agricultural scientist George Washington Carver didn't invent peanut butter to increase his toothless patients' protein intake. He did, however, revolutionize the way people cultivate peanuts, soybeans, and sweet potatoes. The Aztecs and Incas were roasting and grinding peanuts into a paste long before he, Marcellus Gilmore Edson, or even John Harvey Kellogg ever did.

86. Reese's peanut butter chocolate cups were called "penny cups" in the 1930s because they only cost a penny back then... I need a time machine, like, yesterday.

87. Switzerland eats the most chocolate per capita, about 20 pounds (9 kilograms) annually.

88. It takes 400-500 cocoa beans to produce 1 pound (454 grams) of chocolate. A single cacao tree can only produce 3 pounds (1.4 kilograms) worth of chocolate a year.

89. Hershey Kisses got their name because the machine that deposits them onto a conveyor belt makes smooching sounds as it works. 70 million are made daily.

90. Cocoa beans were once used as currency by the Aztecs. Citizens could purchase goods and services, and pay their taxes with cocoa.

91. The Nahuatl-Aztec word for chocolate is "xocolatl," and it means "bitter water." Before the British confectioner Joseph Fry and his son made the first sweet, solid chocolate bar in 1847 by combining sugar, cocoa butter, and cocoa powder, chocolate was only available as a bitter hot drink.

92. The chocolate chip cookie was invented in the 1930s by Ruth Graves Wakefield. When Hershey's offered to buy her recipe, she accepted and asked to be paid with a lifetime supply of chocolate.

93. Well, actually... White chocolate isn't chocolate. It doesn't contain cocoa solids, the things that make chocolate taste like chocolate. It's a mix of milk, sugar, vanilla flavoring, lecithin (which makes food smooth), and cocoa butter.

94. You can thank Michele Ferrero for Ferrero Rocher and Nutella. Thanks to his confections, he became the richest man in Italy and remained so until his passing in 2015. By the way, you know the filling inside Ferrero Rocher? It's Nutella.

95. The Ferrero Group uses 25% of all hazelnuts produced in the world. A 13-ounce (375-gram) jar of Nutella contains around 50 hazelnuts.

96. A new jar of Nutella pops into existence every 2.5 seconds, which is crazy because the average person blinks every 2-4 seconds.

97. Over 365,000 metric tonnes of Nutella are made every year. There is enough Nutella in those jars to wrap around the Earth 1.8 times.

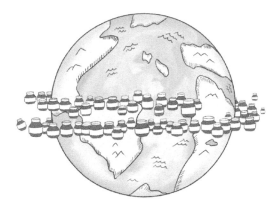

98. Despite the hazelnut confection being an Italian invention, it's the French that consume the most Nutella, an estimated 75,000 metric tonnes annually.

99. One French couple loved the hazelnut spread so much that they tried naming their daughter "Nutella." Luckily, the court didn't indulge them, so they were forced to change their baby girl's name to the more pedestrian "Ella." Thank God. We don't need to give children more reasons to get bullied at school.

100. The popsicle was invented by an 11-year-old boy in 1905. Young Frank Epperson mixed a sugary drink powder in water, forgot about it, and left it outside on a cold night. He came back the next day to a frozen drink with the stirring stick still in it. He called his tasty accident the "epsicle," a combination of his last name and the word "icicle." After he grew up and became a parent, his children suggested he change the name of his epsicle to "popsicle" since he was their pop (father).

Chapter 3

Totally Wild Animal Facts

Hey, you're still reading! It's a good thing, too, because this is probably the best chapter in the whole book. It's definitely our favorite. And you'll soon see why.

It doesn't matter how old you get; animals will always be interesting. Whenever there's an animal on-screen, you can't help but get sucked in and revert to a child, curiously observing their every move, admiring their cuteness, or being astounded by their bewildering behaviors.

Countless myths and legends, documentaries, and art feature animals. Their freedom, beauty, power, and even their unhinged violence has and always will captivate us. Loving animals is human nature.

In this chapter, you'll learn amazing things about the humble chicken, discover little-known facts about your favorite wild animals, uncover the truth about dinosaurs that movies always get wrong, and dig up some cool dog facts.

Sorry cat lovers, but there aren't any feline facts here. Please put your claws away and hold off on the hate mail. I promise cats will be the main animal attraction in the next volume.

***

1. Flamingos feed their babies milk. More specifically, crop milk from their beaks, because birds don't have nipples. They give their chicks predigested food mixed with a secretion from their crop, a pouch on the front of their neck. Penguins and pigeons also make bird milk.

2. Flamingos aren't naturally pink; they're born white or gray and only turn pink after 1-3 years. Their signature hue comes from a beta carotene-rich diet of shrimp and algae. If underfed, they can lose their signature color.

3. Flamingos eat by dipping their heads into near-boiling hot water, then scooping up food with their curved beaks that have built-in strainers. The water is extremely salty, so they get rid of it by snorting it out of their nostrils... So majestic.

4. The "knees" you see on a flamingo are its ankles. The actual knee joints are hidden way up underneath their feathers, close to where the wings attach.

5. A group of flamingos is called a "flamboyance." A group of peacocks is an "ostentation."

6. In most cases, only the male, the peacock, possesses the signature blue and green plumage. Peacocks can also be pink, purple, gray, and white.

7. The peahen is a drab brown so she can easily blend in with her surroundings and raise her peachicks in secret. To keep predators from stealing her eggs, a mother peahen will lay unfertilized decoy eggs in random places.

8. Peacock feathers are called "trains." When chased, they can be detached like a lizard's tail to throw predators off their trail. They grow back, too.

9. Peacocks, turkeys, and chickens are all from the same order, *Galliformes*; they're almost family.

10. Turkeys were once worshiped as gods. This prestigious poultry took part in several Mayan ceremonies and religious rites.

11. Turkeys don't come from the country of Turkey; they're native to the United States. On a side note, there are three towns named Turkey, each in Texas, Louisiana, and North Carolina.

12. Every Thanksgiving, a single turkey is selected by the president of the United States to be spared from the oven and safely retired to a farm, where it is granted immunity from all future human festivities.

13. A male turkey is called a "gobbler." The signature "gobble-gobble" is a mating call. Turkey hens, the females, don't gobble; they cackle.

14. A group of turkeys is called a "gang."

15. The average rooster crow can reach volumes of over 100 decibels, rivaling a jackhammer. To prevent itself from going deaf, the cock will tilt its head back to activate its built-in earplugs.

16. Miracle Mike The Headless Chicken ran around and traveled for 18 months. After being axed, a clot formed that stopped him from bleeding out. To keep the miracle alive, his owner fed him through his throat hole using an eyedropper.

17. The most expensive chicken in the world is the black Ayam Cemani. It costs upwards of $2500. Due to fibromelanosis, this rare Indonesian bird is pitch-black from the inside out, except for its burgundy blood and cream-colored eggs. Its meat stays black when cooked but, disappointingly, it doesn't taste that much better than a regular chicken.

18. Chickens can see in color, remember 100 faces, experience REM sleep and dreams, recognize their names being called like dogs, run around and play with each other, and communicate with their chicks while they're still inside their eggs... Ready to go vegan yet? Me neither.

19. You can hypnotize chickens by placing their beaks on the ground and drawing a straight line in front of them. It works with roosters, too.

20. In 2003, a DNA analysis was done on a 68 million-year-old *T. rex* fossil. It turned out that the humble chicken was the closest genetic match... *T. rex* got nerfed hard!

21. Bhart-Anjan Bhullar, a Harvard student-turned-professor, managed to genetically alter chicken embryos and regress their beaks into dinosaur snouts. He didn't outright say he would build his own dinosaur theme park, but who knows what would happen if he were to take his experiments further.

22. Well, actually... *Tyrannosaurus rex*, *Triceratops*, and *Velociraptor* weren't from the Jurassic period of 200-145 million years ago. They came way later, 145-65 million years ago, during the Cretaceous period.

23. The average lifespan of a *T. rex* is estimated to have been 28 years. Like with a tree stump, each growth ring inside a cross-section of a *T. rex* rib can be counted as a year of life.

24. *T. rex* arms were 3 feet (90 centimeters) long and were so strong they could bench press 400 pounds (180 kilograms) each. Pushups would've been another story, though.

25. Not much else is known about their surprisingly impressive arms, but it's speculated that *T. rex* used them to pin down prey and that males specifically used them to hug their girlfriends so they wouldn't slip off during mating.

26. *T. rex* rubbed their noses together like Eskimo kisses to get in the mood. Be careful where you say "Eskimo." In Alaska and Canada, it's considered a racial slur. Use "Inuit" to avoid getting the cold shoulder. Inuit kisses.

27. The average *T. rex* was 40 feet (12 meters) long snout-to-tail and 13 feet (4 meters) high at the hips —it couldn't stand tall— and weighed as much as 19,555 pounds (9 tonnes). Despite its long and muscular legs, the *T. rex* could only speed walk at a pace of 10 miles per hour (16 kilometers per hour). If it ran fast, it would be crushed under its own weight.

28. Well, actually... The vision of *T. rex* was not dependent on movement. Their orange-sized eyes were quite sharp. Like modern birds of prey, their eyes were forward-facing and had great depth perception. They could see you frozen, shaking with fear from 3.7 miles (6 kilometers) away.

29. Their 60 serrated teeth were quite sharp, too, and could deliver a crushing 12,800 PSI bite. Like crocodiles, they swallowed the chunks they bit off whole, bones and all.

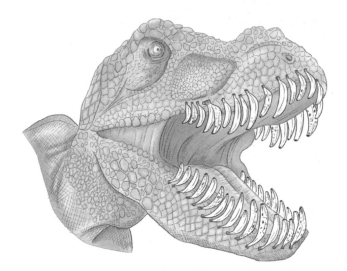

30. The skull of a *T. rex* was 5 feet (1.5 meters) long, and the jaw alone occupied 80% of its length. Its teeth were each the size of bananas, with some even longer.

31. *T. rex* were likely both hunters and scavengers. They would eat anything they could sink their teeth into, even other *T. rex*. They're believed to have been occasional cannibals.

32. Well, actually... The *T. rex* wasn't the largest carnivorous dinosaur. It was the *Spinosaurus*, which outweighed it by a ton. Though the *Spinosaurus* was bigger, it didn't have a strong enough bite to break the thick neck of a *T. rex*. *Spinosaurus'* long, narrow jaw was built for eating fish.

33. Just to flex on the *T. rex*, the *Spinosaurus* had longer arms that let it go from standing on its hind legs to walking on all fours and back whenever it felt like it.

34. Despite both being from the Cretaceous period, *Spinosaurus* and *T. rex* would've never crossed paths. The spined lizard lived in North Africa, and the tyrant lizard king reigned over the US, Canada, and possibly China.

35. The sail on *Spinosaurus'* back was made of long, flat bones that extended from its spine and were covered by webbed skin, a bit like a bat wing. The sail is believed to have regulated its body temperature, but new studies suggest it was more for show. It was more likely a peacock-like display to signal its virility and abundance of food.

36. *Spinosaurus* was the first dinosaur ever to swim. *Plesiosaur*, the creature that inspired the Loch Ness monster, was an aquatic reptile, like the *Mosasaur*.

37. *Mosasaurs* had to come up to get air and gave birth to live young underwater like whales, which are mammals, do.

38. The largest *Mosasaur* likely couldn't have been more than 50 feet (15 meters) or have been able to jump out of the water and drag down bioengineered monstrosities. Their fossilized stomach contents reveal that they ate fish, turtles, *Plesiosaurs*, ammonites, and seafaring birds.

39. Well, actually... The so-called *Velociraptors* in the *Jurassic Park* movie franchise aren't *Velociraptors* at all; they're *Deinonychus*. It's unlikely they're *Utahraptors* because *Utahraptors* are much longer from snout-to-tail.

40. Real *Velociraptors* weren't much taller than a domestic turkey and had plenty of feathers to boot. The human-sized *Deinonychus* also had some plumage.

41. Both *Velociraptor* and *Deinonychus* would use the long sickle-like claws on their big toes to stab at the soft bellies of herbivores. After the assault, they would withdraw and wait for their prey to pass out from blood loss.

42. Paleontologists believe that the prehistoric raptors' claws may have also been used to climb trees and as a display structure to attract mates.

43. *Velociraptors* often preyed on *Protoceratops*, which were the horn-less, pig-sized relatives of *Triceratops*. A fossil of the enemies locked in eternal combat was found in Mongolia.

44. Well, actually... *Velociraptors* didn't hunt in packs and weren't smart enough to launch coordinated assaults or set traps... A "clever girl," she wasn't.

45. Like their raptor ancestors, cassowaries possess huge 5-inch (13-centimeter) talons that cut through flesh like a hot knife on butter. These modern dinosaurs fight by jumping 7 feet (over 2 meters) in the air and slashing at their enemy. Imagine an angry kangaroo coming at you with knives strapped to its feet.

46. Cassowaries are the deadliest birds in the world and, as such, are nicknamed "murderbirds." Though they attack 100-200 people yearly, they never do it without provocation. On nearly every occasion, it was because a human approached them first. Only 2 people have been con-firmed to have died at the hands —feet— of a cassowary.

47. Cassowaries are mainly frugivores (fruit eaters) but do partake in the occasional rodent, reptile, or pile of dung. These birds aren't good at digesting fruit, so plenty of good nutrition is still left in their droppings, which they or other cassowaries don't let go to waste. This habit helps spread seeds and restore trees.

48. The true purpose of the crest, or casque, on the cassowary's head is unknown. Experts believe it's used as either a mating display, a helmet during fights, a sound booster to better project its deep bellows, or all of the above.

49. Well, actually… *Dilophosaurus*, the dog-sized dinosaur that dispatched the overweight programmer in Jurassic Park, couldn't spit poison, had no frilled neck that it could flare out, and was 20 feet (6 meters) long.

50. The skull of a *Triceratops* occupies a third of its massive 30-foot (9-meter) frame. The largest skull found so far measured an impressive 8.2 feet (2.5 meters).

51. The frill of a *Triceratops*, also known as a "flounce," was likely used as a shield, for temperature regulation, for communication, and, of course, as a mating display.

52. *Triceratops* weren't fast enough to outrun *T. rex*, which preyed upon them, but what they lacked in speed, they made up for it with their size and weapons. Their top 2 horns grew to 3 feet (90 centimeters) or more, and they had sharp, parrot-like beaks that could tear *T. rex* a new one.

53. Even if we could extract viable dinosaur DNA from amber-preserved mosquitoes, frog DNA wouldn't be enough to fill the gaps needed to clone dinosaurs.

54. Some frogs, like the African reed frogs, can change their sex in adulthood. It was thought that this would only happen in polluted waters, but new research suggests that sequential hermaphroditism can occur even in pristine waters.

55. Frogs and toads fertilize externally, without intercourse during mating. The male latches onto the female's back, lines up his cloaca with hers, then fertilizes as the female ejects her eggs. This is called "amplexus," also known as "froggy style."

56. After mating, the male Surinam toad pushes the fertilized eggs onto the female's back. Up to 100 eggs fuse into her skin. When they have developed into mini-toads, they pop out of their mother's back like pimples. Ah, the miracle of birth... If it's any consolation, dear readers, its scientific name is "pipa pipa," and it looks like a waffle with eyes.

57. If you put a frog in a pot of cool water, then very gradually turn up the heat, it will most certainly notice and try to jump out, just like if you were to put it in already boiling water.

58. This or that? Frogs versus toads. Frogs have long back legs for jumping, webbed feet, teeth on their upper jaw, and lay eggs in clusters that resemble a bunch of grapes. Toads, however, have short, stubby legs for crawling on dirt, little to no webbing on their feet, no teeth, and lay eggs in long strands resembling Mardi Gras beads.

59. The poison of a golden dart frog is strong enough to wipe out 10 grown men. Just brushing your arm against it is enough to do you in. Within 10 minutes of contact, you will feel numb, your heart will shut down, and you will stop breathing. Use that time wisely to pray to your God or Gods for a pleasant afterlife because there is no antidote for batrachotoxin.

60. The Choco Emberá tribe of the Panama rainforest rub golden dart frog poison onto their arrow tips to hunt and defend themselves. Even outside the frog's body, the toxin is still potent for at least 2 years after application.

61. Golden dart frogs get their poison by eating a mix of ants, termites, centipedes, and beetles, absorbing and concentrating toxins over their lifetime. A dead golden dart frog can still be very dangerous if touched bare-handed.

62. Well, actually... Toads and frogs don't give you warts. HPV does. "Human Papillomavirus, as the name implies, is transmitted between humans. You still shouldn't handle them because the oil from your hands hurts their delicate skin.

63. A group of frogs is called an "army," or a "chorus." A group of toads is a "knot" or a "nest."

64. This or that? The difference between poison and venom in animals is that venom is actively injected through fangs, spikes, or stingers, while poison is passive. Poison is usually on an animal's skin, scales, feathers, or in its organs and muscles. So long as you don't touch or bite it, you probably won't get poisoned.

65. The fastest snake on earth is the black mamba. It can maintain a slithering speed of up to 12 miles per hour (19 kilometers per hour).

66. Although a black mamba can inject 12 times the lethal dose and put you in a body bag in just 15 hours or less, it's not the deadliest. Cobras and saw-scaled vipers take out the most people.

67. The WHO estimates that up to 138,000 people die of snakebites every year worldwide. India and similar developing countries get the worst of it.

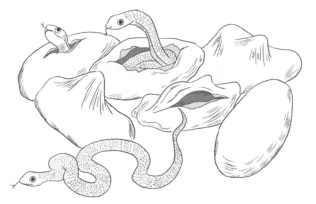

68. Snake eggs are leathery and stretchy, not brittle like chicken eggs. Not all snakes are oviparous, though. Some snakes like anacondas, boa constrictors, and sea snakes give live births just like mammals do.

69. The smallest snake in the world is the Barbados thread snake. It's only 4 inches (10 centimeters) long and as thin as a strand of spaghetti.

70. The longest snake in the world ever recorded was a reticulated python shot in 1912 in Indonesia. It measured 32 feet 9.5 inches (10 meters)... That's one danger noodle that would slurp you right up.

71. The average snake can open its jaw 150° wide, but the boomslang snake can gape its mouth to 170°.

72. Snakes will burst if they bite off more than they can chew, err... swallow. In 2005, a python was found torn in half after trying to eat an alligator in the Florida Everglades. Officials didn't make it in time to rescue the poor gator.

73. Snakes can and do swallow humans whole. A 25-year-old farmer was eaten in 2017, and a 54-year-old was devoured the following year. Both incidents happened in Indonesia, and footage of the crime scenes may still be found online.

74. In 2009, an African farmer fended off a hungry python for 3 hours. He managed to get his shirt off and covered the 12-foot (3.7-meter) python's mouth. During the skirmish, he managed to call the police on his cellphone and was rescued.

75. Sonoran coral snakes scare off predators by farting on them. They can flatulate on command by sucking in air through their cloaca and loudly expelling it... Cool party trick.

76. When threatened, the cobra will regurgitate its meal to make a quick escape. If there is no escape, it can poop on command to deter persistent predators.

77. A group of rattlesnakes is called a "rhumba." Dancing the rhumba would be the last thing on my mind if I were to find myself in a pit of snakes.

78. Well, actually... Rattlesnake rattles don't have little pebbles inside them like maracas. The noise is made by the layers of hard tissue hitting and scraping against each other at very high speeds. These snakes can rattle their tails 50-100 times a second and for up to 2 hours, non-stop.

79. Rattlesnake rattles are made of keratin, the same material as your nails.

80. Baby rattlesnakes can't rattle their tails. Only after 2 layers, also known as "buttons," are formed can a young serpent earn its namesake. It usually doesn't grow past 12 buttons.

81. Snakes flick their tongues to smell the air for prey, predators, and mates. They stick their tongue out to catch scents, retract it, then rub the odor particles that stuck onto it against the Jacobson's organ, the smell processing unit located on the roof of their mouth.

82. The tongues of snakes, and some lizards, are forked because it lets them know the direction a smell is coming from. If the scent is more intense on the right fork, the reptile knows its source is toward that specific side. It's similar to how your ears can tell if a sound is coming from the left or right.

83. You probably wouldn't hear an elephant sneaking behind you. Its feet have thick, fatty pads that absorb impact and spread out its weight, dampening sound. Elephants can hear through their feet, picking up vibrations from the ground.

84. The African elephant is the largest land animal in the world, weighing a whopping 6 tonnes and towering over the animal kingdom at 10 feet (3 meters) high. Given their massive bodies, elephants can't jump.

85. Well, actually... Elephants aren't afraid of mice, but they will go out of their way to avoid a king cobra, whose venom is potent enough to fell a fully-grown elephant. They are also averse to bees. Farmers line the perimeter of their farms with beehives to keep elephants from parading all over their crops.

86. Like little children sucking their thumbs, elephants will soothe themselves by sucking on their trunks when feeling distressed, sometimes even as adults. When they need to be comforted, they wrap their trunks together with another elephant.

87. Elephant trunks weigh 400 pounds (180 kilograms) and have more than 40,000 individual muscles in them. They are strong enough to lift tree trunks but delicate enough to pluck out a single blade of grass. This is thanks to the finger-like projections located on the edges of their nostrils.

88. Elephant tusks are humongous front teeth, not low-hanging horns, as you may have thought. Like beavers, elephant tusks/teeth will keep growing as long as they're alive. Because of these pearly whites, 90% of the African elephant population has been decimated by poachers for the illegal ivory trade.

89. This or that? Besides being bigger than their Asian cousins, African elephants have larger ears that resemble the continent of Africa. What also distinguishes African elephants is that they have 2 finger-like projections at the end of their trunks, while their Asian cousins have one.

ASIAN   AFRICAN

90. A group of elephants is called a "memory." It's also called a "parade."

91. Elephant mothers can expect a 22-month gestation period —the longest of any mammal. The newborn elephant exits the womb and enters the world at a staggering 265 pounds (120 kilograms)... I feel sorry for the momma elephant.

92. With their massive 12-pound (5.4-kilogram) brains, elephants indeed never forget. Even from a brief encounter, they can remember other elephants and humans, poachers especially, and keep fond memories or hold grudges for life.

93. The matriarch elephant, the leader, has the best memory of them all. She can recall multiple routes, the location of watering holes, and even time the herd's arrival to past feeding grounds to coincide with the ripening of specific fruit.

94. Well, actually... Elephants don't see humans as cute the way we do with puppies. The internet lied. Gasp. Wild elephants know what humans are capable of and see us as legitimate threats. Tame elephants raised in captivity can develop trust and feel affection toward their handlers.

95. Hippopotamuses, rhinoceroses, and elephants are classified as pachyderms, large land mammals with thick hides. Despite that, hippos are more closely related to whales and dolphins than to the other pachyderms.

96. Hippos can hold their breaths for 5 minutes. When sleeping in water, they'll automatically resurface every few minutes, like dolphins.

97. Hippos can sprint on land at 30 miles per hour (48 kilometers per hour). They're faster than Usain Bolt.

98. Young hippopotamuses play tag by running after and slamming into each other in the water. If you get hit, you're it... I'll pass.

99. Hippos make their own moisturizer and sunblock called "blood sweat." The deep red hipposudoric acid, often mistaken for blood, comes out of the hippo's pores and mixes with clear, watery sweat to form pink sweat.

100. Well, actually... Hippo milk isn't pink; it's white-yellow. Hippo calves can suckle on land and underwater by closing their eyes, ears, and nostrils.

101. Though they're herbivores, hippos have 20-inch (50-centimeter) long canines, can open their mouths 150-180° wide, and have a bite force of 1,800 PSI. It's about half of a crocodile's bite, but more than enough to bite a croc in half.

102. Hippopotamuses kill 500 people in Africa every year. They're fiercely territorial and attack anything that gets near them, even boats. It's not uncommon for adult males to drown baby hippos that venture into their domain... Not so cute now, are they?

103. Hippos mark their territories by propelling poop and wagging their tail like an upside-down windshield wiper to spread it out.

104. "Hippopotamus" means "river horse" in Greek. A group of these river horses is a "bloat." They don't float and can't swim; they sink and walk underwater until they reach land.

105. African rhinoceros are horrible swimmers that have been known to drown in deep enough water. To cool off, they roll around in the mud. Their Asian cousins, however, are excellent swimmers.

106. Between the blacks, the whites, the Indians, the Sumatrans, and the Javans, the white rhino is the largest of the lot, weighing over 7,715 pounds (3.5 tonnes). Sources vary on whether the white rhinoceros or common hippopotamus is heavier, but most often, the white rhino wins the heavyweight championship.

107. According to the International Rhino Foundation, only 28,000 rhinos exist in the world. Most notably, there are only 80 or fewer Sumatrans and just 74 Javans.

108. Powdered rhino horn is used as a cure-all and aphrodisiac in Asia, even though it's bunk. Rhino horn is also a highly sought-after status symbol in the black market.

109. Well, actually... Rhino horns aren't made of bone. They're made of densely compacted layers of keratin, the same thing your hair and nails are made of. Their horns can grow up to 79 inches (200 centimeters).

110. Rhinos communicate with each other through snorts, squeaks, sneezes, urine, and feces... That's one heated debate I wouldn't want to be a part of.

111. A group of rhinoceros is called a "crash." "Rhinoceros," "rhinoceroses," and "rhinoceri," are all acceptable plurals.

112. Rhinos are nervous creatures and have terrible eyesight. As a precaution, they will charge at any moving object within 100 feet (30 meters) of them. Their poor vision is dependent on movement, but they can smell and hear you.

113. Coyotes sneakily walk on their tiptoes to avoid being heard when ambushing. No, they don't hunt rhinoceros, if you're wondering.

114. Not many animals dare to eat a porcupine, but coyotes are very cunning —or very desperate— creatures. They can coordinate themselves in pairs or packs to overwhelm the spiked rodent. Their strategy: distract it, flip it over, and pin it down to expose its bare belly for the killing bite.

115. Well, actually... Coyotes don't need traps to catch roadrunners. Coyotes can run at 40 miles per hour (64 kilometers per hour), double the speed of the roadrunner.

116. Roadrunners pair up to hunt snakes. One bird distracts the serpent from the front while the other bird pins its head from behind and then mercilessly slams it on a rock. It's a good thing they're small.

117. Roadrunners are cousins to cuckoo birds. They both have four toes that leave x-shaped prints, which make it hard for predators to track them on the ground.

118. Common cuckoos don't incubate or raise young in their own nests. They're brood parasites that go into other birds' nests, throw out one egg, and sneak in one of theirs in its place. The unsuspecting host parents then rear the invader's brood as if it were their own.

119. Female cuckoos lay one egg at a time in up to 25 different host nests every breeding season. Each type of cuckoo egg looks very similar to the specific hosts', and some cuckoo chicks even grow feathers that resemble the hosts' chicks.

120. The parasitic cuckoo chick will squawk louder to make the forced foster parents feed it instead of their own chicks. While the parents aren't looking, the freeloader will push its foster siblings (hatched or not) out of the nest.

121. Only adult males make the "cuckoo" sound. The females make bubbling noises.

122. Cuckoo clocks were most likely invented in the Black Forest region of Germany in the 1600s by farmers to make ends meet during the harsh winter. Their signature sound is made by a mechanism that pumps air through two tiny whistles. Each "cuckoo" represents an hour, so six "cuckoos" means it's six o'clock.

123. This or that? The quickest way to tell a wild coyote, wolf, or dog apart without getting too close for comfort is to look at their tail while they're running. Coyotes keep their tails down, wolves keep them straight behind them, and dogs curl their tails up while darting about.

124. Coyotes can interbreed with dogs and wolves. Hybrids are called "coydogs" and "coywolves." In Newfoundland, Canada, there are snow-white coydogs.

125. Arctic foxes can withstand a blistering cold -94°F (-70°C) without breaking a sweat. These white foxes shed their coats in the spring and turn brown or gray.

126. Like fluffy little missiles, arctic foxes can pinpoint an animal's location under the snow using the Earth's magnetic field as a guide, then nosedive onto their target.

127. Gray foxes are more cat than dog. They have eyes with slit pupils and long whiskers on their face, are most active at night, climb trees, and can retract their claws at will.

128. Fennec foxes are the size of kittens and have densely furred paws to walk on hot desert sands. Their adorably large ears help dissipate heat.

129. Foxes have been selectively bred and successfully domesticated in Russia since around 1959. You can import a mail order Russian fox for the low, low price of just $9,000.

130. What does the fox say? A lot of things. It barks, howls, yips, trills, gekkers, screams, and shrieks, among other things. The domesticated foxes even laugh.

131. A fox pup is called a "kit," a female is a "vixen," and a male is a "tod." A group of foxes is called a "leash," "skulk," or "earth."

132. Mother vixens sometimes get help from their sisters or older daughters to raise their litter of up to 11 kits. The helpers gain valuable parenting experience for when it's their turn to rear a family.

133. Dingoes can rotate their heads a full 180° to look behind themselves, and their wrists can rotate like ours to catch prey, climb trees, and turn door knobs.

134. Dingoes can and, in fact, have attacked babies. It's been confirmed that little Azaria Chamberlain was taken by a dingo in 1980. At the time, the mother, Lindy Chamberlain, was falsely charged with the murder of her child and given a life sentence. The father, Michael Chamberlain, was wrongly accused of being an accessory and sentenced to 18 months. Fortunately, they were eventually proven innocent and freed.

135. The darkly comedic "A dingo ate my baby!" was inspired by *A Cry in the Dark*, a 1988 Australian film based on the event, with Meryl Streep as the lead.

136. Australians built a wall to keep illegal dingoes out. The fence wall currently stretches 3488 miles (5614 kilometers) but used to be longer. It costs taxpayers in Australia $10 million AUD annually to maintain it.

137. Of the four hyena species, only the spotted hyena makes laughing sounds; the striped, brown, and aardwolf species don't.

138. Well, actually... Spotted hyenas don't "laugh" to express joy. It's the opposite. They giggle when hunting, fleeing, and fighting with each other.

139. A group of hyenas is called a "cackle." A single cackle can have up to 80 hyenas.

140. Hyenas are better at cooperating and solving problems together than chimpanzees... And likely humans, I'd wager.

141. Female spotted hyenas have three times more testosterone than males and possess deeper voices. The lower the pitch, the older and more dominant she is.

142. Spotted hyenas have a strict matriarchal social structure. Full-grown males are automatically ranked lower than female pups. When males leave their cackle for a new one, they're ruthlessly hazed by the females before being considered as potential mates.

143. Hyenas aren't just scavengers; they're also hunters, often more successful than lions. Being opportunistic creatures, though, hyenas won't hesitate to save themselves the trouble of hunting by chasing a pride of lions away from their kill.

144. Spotted hyenas have a bite force of 1,100 PSI, double that of a lion's 650. Additionally, some tests measured the bite of a gray wolf to be 1,200 PSI strong.

145. The terms "alpha male" and "beta male" are no longer used by wolf experts to describe the dominant and submissive males of the pack. Male wolves don't usually compete with each other to be top dog. The boys become men by mating with females from other packs and starting their own families.

146. A wolf can wolf down 20 pounds (9 kilograms) of meat in a single meal. That's 100 cheeseburgers in human terms.

147. Wolves can swim for 8 miles (13 kilometers). Ironman triathletes can only swim for 2.4 miles (3.9 kilometers).

148. If a wolf is not pulling its weight by helping raise the pups or is constantly fumbling hunts, it can sometimes get kicked out of the pack and/or killed. As a result, lone wolves howl less often to avoid detection.

149. A wolf would make a terrible guard dog. Wolves go out of their way to not physically interact with humans, and upon encountering someone or something new when on their own, their first instinct would be to flee rather than fight.

150. Well, actually... Wolves don't howl at the Moon. It looks like they do because they're most active at night, and howling upwards projects the sound better for pack members to hear each other over long distances. Wolves have been observed howling in the daytime.

151. Wolf howls are a language. They're used to relay location, inform the pack that prey has been found or captured, and tell rival packs to stay away. Much like drunk humans singing show tunes, wolves bond by howling together. Members of the pack can recognize each other's specific voice.

152. If you howl like a wolf, a real wolf will howl back at you. The International Wolf Center in Ely, Minnesota, holds contests to see who is the best human howler.

153. Dire wolves existed until 13,000 years ago, but they were not just oversized wolves. A 2021 study published in the Nature journal explains that these ancient wolves split from their shared genetic ancestor 5.7 million years ago. Dire wolves and regular wolves were so different they couldn't have interbred.

154. The tallest dog breed in the world is the Irish wolfhound, a gentle giant —gentle towards humans, at least— that stands about 35 inches tall (90 centimeters) at the shoulders.

155. Dogs most likely evolved from the gray wolf at least 15,000 years ago. The first clear-cut case of dog domestication was about 14,200 years ago in the form of the Bonn-Oberkassel dog fossil found in ancient Germany.

156. Dogs like squeaky toys because they remind them of the high-pitched cries of an injured animal. Thanks to their wolven origins, dogs have an ancient hunting instinct that compels them to tear apart and thrash around things that resemble or smell like prey they would find in the wild.

157. Well, actually... Dogs don't see the world in black-and-white. Though they only possess one-fifth of the color-sensing cone cells we have and are colorblind to the red-green spectrum, they can see shades of gray, blue, and yellow.

158. Dogs don't have sweat glands under their skin. They sweat through their paws. Their tongues also help dissipate heat, which is why dogs pant.

159. Dogs have wet noses because it helps them catch more scent molecules and smell better. Dog and cat noses have unique prints, just like human fingers.

160. Dogs' noses are 100,000 times more sensitive than ours. They can be trained to predict epileptic episodes, detect changes in blood sugar levels of diabetics, and sniff out breast, bladder, prostate, and skin cancers through human urine.

161. Chocolate is deadly to dogs because they can't process the theobromine in it. This chemical causes toxic shock, seizures, fever, diarrhea, and vomiting. A stray chocolate chip might be ok, but a bar of 70% cacao can make your dog go to heaven.

162. Dogs instinctively align themselves with the Earth's magnetic field when pooping. They prefer to go north or south, but almost never east or west. This may explain why your dog takes forever to poop sometimes; it's calibrating its internal compass in response to the subtle changes of the Earth's constantly shifting magnetic field.

163. Dogs are hardwired to recognize and imitate the facial expressions of humans. And they can sometimes take on their owners' personalities. It's not your imagination when you see a dog that resembles its owner.

164. Well, actually... According to research findings at the Barnard College in New York, dogs can't express guilt. Your woofer will slump and stare at you with those puppy dog eyes regardless of whether they did something wrong or not. That "guilty" dog look is them reacting to your negative reaction. They know you're displeased with them but don't quite understand why, so they act submissively by default.

165. Border collies, the most intelligent dog breed, can understand and recognize up to 200 words. Their intelligence is comparable to that of a 3-year-old child.

166. Stray dogs in Moscow, Russia, ride the subway to get around the city. They recognize specific stops and remember which locations have food.

167. Dalmatians are born all-white. Their black spots develop as they mature.

168. The longest a dog ever lived was 29 years and 5 months. Bluey, an Australian cattle dog, barked from 1910 to 1939.

169. Labrador retrievers were bred to "retrieve" ducks their owners shot down from the water. Their webbed paws and thick rudder-like tails, sometimes called "otter tails," make them good swimmers.

170. Welsh corgis were originally cattle herders. Their small stature allows them to nip at cows' ankles without getting kicked in retaliation.

171. Weiner dogs were selectively bred to have short legs and narrow, tubular bodies to go into badger dens and drag them out, hence the name "dachshund," which means "badger dog" in German.

172. Basset hounds, corgis, dachshunds, and Pekingese have short legs because of a genetic defect called "achondroplastic dwarfism." In short, the parts of their limbs that are supposed to grow until adulthood stop growing in puppyhood.

173. Because of their long body shape and stubby legs, dwarf dogs are prone to back injuries and slipped discs. Confoundingly, munchkins, the wiener dogs of the cat world, have no more spine issues than the regular domestic feline.

174. The pooch we commonly call a pit bull is specifically an American pit bull terrier. "Pit bull" is also used for American Staffordshire terriers, Staffordshire bull terriers, or any dog that is a mix of the breeds mentioned.

175. Well, actually... Pit bulls were never nanny dogs. The first pit bulls were bred for the express purpose of biting and restraining bulls and then canine mortal combat.

176. Pit bulls have come a long way. They score an 82.3% passing rate on the American Temperament Test Society's dog behavior evaluation. In terms of friendliness, emotional stability, and loyalty, modern pit bulls are top dogs.

177. Well, actually... Electric eels are a type of knife fish, more related to catfish than to real eels. These electric fishes have to come up for air every 10 minutes.

178. Electric eels can discharge 600-860 volts of electricity, but the jolt isn't often strong enough to injure humans. There are very few documented cases.

179. Electric eels can accidentally shock themselves. Their slick skin and the thick layer of fat under it help dissipate the current, thus minimizing the damage.

180. Electric eels are good fathers. When protecting their young fry from predators, they will tell their offspring to hide in their mouths, as this is the safest place when they're making sparks fly. Shock-noodle daddies and babies communicate with each other using low-voltage pulses.

Chapter 4

Nature and Plant Matters of Fact

I love nature, which is why I live in the city, isolate myself in my condo with the curtains shut and write facts about it.

The beauty and power of nature have fascinated humans since time immemorial. Until scientists came along, we thought that mundane things like trees, lakes, rain, lightning, and tornadoes were the work of gods or the gods themselves. Unlike many other things in life, even though nature lost its mystery, it hasn't lost its magic.

In this chapter, you will learn amazing things about everyday weather events that you probably never think twice about and discover extraordinary natural phenomena that you thought were impossible.

If you're more of a lover of plants and flowers, stick around because you might just pick up a helpful thing or two. And if you live in a concrete jungle or don't care in the slightest about gardening, give this chapter a chance, still. Plants are actually cool. They're not just boring green things that stand there and take everyone's crap... Unless it's manure. Plants love manure.

***

1. Only 15% of all plant species live on land. The remaining 85% are aquatic. Seaweed and algae make up a large part of it.

2. An areola is a space between the veins of a leaf.

3. The soothing scent of cut grass is caused by a stress response. When under attack, grass releases volatile chemicals to fight off threats and warn other grass that there is danger nearby... Oh, the irony. Even if they are alerted by the death screams of their fallen comrades, it's not like grass can outrun a lawnmmower.

4. There is grass that is tall enough to hide an elephant. It measures 10-23 feet (3-7 meters) in height. It's called "elephant grass" because they love to eat it, blowing their cover in the process.

5. The tallest grass is the Dragon bamboo. It can reach an absurd height of up to 115 feet (35 meters).

6. Burmese bamboo is the fastest growing land plant in the world. This member of the grass family grows up to 35 inches (90 centimeters) each day until it reaches a maximum height of 82 feet (25 meters). It's rivaled only by giant sea kelp.

7. Sunflowers grow up to 30 feet (9 meters) tall.

8. Each petal on a sunflower is a flower itself, and within a sunflower's brown head, there are thousands of tiny flowers called "florets." It's a flower-ception.

9. Sunflower seeds come from the head, where the florets bloom and mature. The seeds are harvested by rubbing off the seeds into a bucket or container.

10. Well, actually... Not all sunflowers are yellow. Some are red, white, or purple.

11. Despite their bold, beautiful colors, sunflowers don't smell like flowers. Their smell is said to be faintly resinous or slightly like honey.

12. Sunflowers face east at sunrise and follow the Sun as it sets west. Overnight they turn themselves back to the east to meet the Sun the following morning.

13. Tulips were worth more than gold in the 17th century. In the Netherlands, the bulbs were used as currency, and the Dutch were obsessed with them. Some historians blame Tulipmania for causing the Dutch economy to crash, though it is debatable.

14. Striped tulips, the multicolored kind, are called "broken tulips." They're illegal in the Netherlands because they spread a deadly virus that affects ordinary tulips.

15. According to Holland.com —an actual website— the country's official name is the Kingdom of the Netherlands. Though "Holland" is used interchangeably with "the Netherlands," the word "Holland" pertains to only 2 of the Netherlands' 12 provinces, Noord-Holland and Zuid-holland.

16. You shouldn't plant daffodils next to tulips or roses because when the daffodils' stems are cut, their mucilage (slime) can get on other flowers and suffocate them.

17. People with good gardening skills are said to have a green thumb. Those that can't garden to save their life have a brown thumb.

18. Despite being the Dutch national flower, tulips are not native to the Netherlands. They were imported in the late 16th century from Turkey.

19. Tulips can talk. If you want them to say "I love you," give your beloved red tulips. To say "I'm sorry," give your significant other white tulips, and pray they forgive you for forgetting your anniversary was last week.

20. Snapdragons got their name because their flowers resemble the head of a dragon. If you squeeze a snapdragon flower from the sides, its petals will open and close like a mouth. Snapdragons are also called "lion's lips" in the Dutch language.

21. As winter approaches, the snapdragon's pretty little flowers wilt and morph into macabre skulls... Dude, that's so metal!

22. The smallest flower and the smallest fruit come from watermeal, *Wolffia spp.*, aka "duckweed." This aquatic plant is barely the size of a round donut sprinkle.

23. Nature's largest single flower is the *Rafflesia arnoldi*. This red and white dotted plant can grow 3.3 feet (1 meter) wide and weigh up to 24 pounds (11 kilograms). Its aroma resembles rotting meat. It's the second most famous corpse flower.

24. Unlike most plants, Rafflesia doesn't have its own roots or stems. It's a parasitic plant that burrows into the Tetrastigma vine tree, a member of the grape family, *Vitaceae*. From the time it infects the vine tree, the Rafflesia takes nine months to flower and only stays in bloom for a week at most.

25. The titan arum, the other corpse flower, is the world's tallest flowering plant. This smelly beast of a flower can reach up to 20 feet (6 meters) in height. Talk about a big stink... No? Nothing? Okay... Moving on to the next fact.

26. Despite its smell, this corpse flower is not easy to find. It only blooms once every 7-10 years, for just 24-48 hours each time.

27. The titan arum, like a sunflower, is a cluster of smaller flowers that make up a much larger structure, called an "inflorescence."

28. The scientific name of the titan arum is *Amorphophallus titanum*, which means "giant misshapen phallus." Eww.

29. To better project its ghastly stench, this fetid phallic flower warms itself to 98°F (36.6°C), roughly the same temperature as a freshly deceased human body. Ugh.

30. Both the Rafflesia and the titan arum emit a carrion-like bouquet to trick flies and beetles into visiting them. These bugs like to plant their eggs into rotting meat, their food of choice, so their hungry babies can eat right after hatching. Once the hopeful bug parents go inside the cadaver flowers and find no cadavers present, they leave with pollen attached to their bodies, doing the dirty work of spreading the plants' offspring across the land.

31. The Mexican Giant Cardon can live for 300 years and grow to a ridiculous 66 feet (20 m). It's the tallest of all cacti.

32. Well, actually... If you run out of water in the desert, it's a terrible idea to get hydration from the first cactus you see. Their plump leaves contain a thick gel that you can't extract drinkable water from through normal means. Cutting the top of just any ol' any cactus is also a big no-no because ingesting the toxic fluid inside can induce vomiting and/or diarrhea, dehydrating you beyond salvation.

33. No cactus is 100% safe to drink, but survivalists say that the fishhook barrel, a stout cactus with long curved spikes, can be used as a last resort. Please consult with an expert before poking a straw into a cactus.

34. The hallucinogenic compound in the peyote cactus is mescaline. It causes intensified emotions, feelings of spiritual enlightenment, and kaleidoscopic vision. Members of The Peyote Way Church of God are permitted by the state of Arizona to use the plant for religious ceremonies... I think it's high time I joined a new religion.

35. The cultivation of peyote is legal in Texas. Prospecting growers must register with the Federal Drug Enforcement Agency for a license.

36. A man was once killed by a cactus. In 1982 in Arizona, David Grundman shot at a 27-foot (8-meter) saguaro —the iconic cactus with arms featured in every western— and was both crushed and impaled by a thorny arm that he broke off with the blast... Boards don't hit back, but cacti do.

37. Cacti at the Saguaro National Park have microchips embedded in them to track their location. There are thieves that sneak into the park and saw off the cacti to sell them on the black market.

38. This or that? Though used interchangeably, succulents and cacti aren't the same thing. Succulents are the main plant category, and cacti are a subcategory of succulents. In general, succulents are smooth with multiple thick leaves that are sometimes arranged like flower petals. Their leaves have short points along the edges or a single point on the tips. Cacti are often flat, cylindrical, or ball-shaped, and have bumps (areoles) that spikes jut out of like needles on a pincushion.

39. Agave, the plant used for tequila and mezcal production, for example, is a succulent but not a cactus. Succulents and cacti are a bit like whisky, in a sense. Not every whisky is a bourbon, but every bourbon is a whisky. Whisky is the umbrella term and bourbon, along with scotch, is a specific type of whisky, "whiskey" with an "e," if you're Irish or American.

40. There are 600 known species of oak trees. They can thrive all over the world, even on sandy beaches.

41. Oak trees get struck by lightning more often than any other tree.

42. The oak is the national tree of the United States, United Kingdom, and Germany. Oaks are a symbol of strength and longevity.

43. An Oak anniversary is when a couple has been married for 80 years.

44. Oak trees can live for up to 1,000 years and make up to 10 million acorns in their lifetime. After reaching maturity at 20-50 years of age, they produce 2,000 acorns annually, but only 1 out of 10,000 acorns make it into treehood. Only 1,000 of mother oak's babies survive; it's sad, really.

45. The tallest living tree is a colossal coast redwood that towers 380 feet (116 meters) high. This California giant is named Hyperion, after the Greek titan. Its exact location is undisclosed for fear of overtourism and the damage that would ensue.

46. The oldest tree in existence is a nearly 5,000-year-old bristlecone pine. Methuselah the tree also lives in California, and its location is also a secret. It got its name from the biblical figure said to have lived for nearly a millennium.

47. 400 million years ago, long before tall trees and dinosaurs existed, 26-foot (8-meter) tall mushrooms called "prototaxites" ruled the world.

48. The Oregon giant honey mushroom is the largest organism in existence. It stretches 2,385 acres, which is equal to 1,350 soccer fields, or "football" fields for you Europeans out there. The giant honey mushroom also glows in the dark.

49. The Great Barrier Reef of Australia is the largest living structure on Earth. This gargantuan coral is made of several interconnected reefs, and it spans over 1,250 miles (2,000 kilometers).

50. The iconic red and white mushroom in Super Mario is based on the Amanita muscaria (aka the fly agaric), a psychedelic mushroom that distorts your sense of size and makes you think you are a giant... It all makes sense now.

51. Mushrooms of the magic variety, which contain the hallucinogenic chemical psilocybin, are shown to be safe and effective in the treatment of PTSD when used under medical supervision.

52. When comparing the various substances people willingly poison themselves with, Mary Jane and mushrooms are the least dangerous recreational drugs. They're significantly safer than even alcohol or tobacco... For the record, I'm not encouraging the use of any substance; I'm just stating facts.

53. The consumption of magical mushrooms has been practiced as far back as 4,000 years ago or more. Ancient Mesoamerican civilizations like the Mayans and Aztecs were fond of making mushroom-themed sculptures.

54. Mushrooms sometimes sprout together in perfect circles called "fairy rings." You can usually see them in the woods during the late summer to early fall after it rains.

55. Terrence McKenna's Stoned Ape theory suggests that we acquired bigger, smarter brains because our ancestors stumbled upon psilocybin mushrooms and ate them. Once ridiculed by the scientific community, his theory is now being taken seriously by mushroom expert Paul Stamets and a handful of other big-brains.

56. Human DNA is closer genetically to mushrooms than it is to plants. Though mushrooms are considered vegetables in the culinary sense, they're actually fungi, similar to the yeast used in breadmaking... We're all walking, talking mushrooms.

57. Siberian reindeer intentionally eat magic mushrooms to get stoned. In the absence of mushrooms, they will seek out the urine of other reindeer, which contains traces of the drug. Reindeer won't hesitate to fight each other over a yellow snow cone.

58. Land that is struck with lightning grows more mushrooms. Experimental Japanese farmers electrocute their crops to yield more plentiful mushroom harvests.

59. When lightning strikes a beach or any sandy surface, small glass-like tubes called "fulgurite" are formed. Fulgurite is one of the rarest stones on Earth, and both scientists and jewelers pay top dollar for it.

60. Well, actually... Lightning does strike the same place twice, and many, many more times than that. Lightning bolts strike the Earth up to 100 times a second. That equals 8,000,000 times per day and 3,000,000,000 times every year.

61. The Empire State Building gets electrocuted at least 25 times every year.

62. It's not uncommon for airplanes to get struck by lightning. Don't worry; they're built to withstand multiple lightning bolts and keep flying.

63. Lightning storms occur most often in the late afternoon or early evening, but they can happen even if the sky is bright and blue and there are no clouds or rain in sight. If you ever hear a thunderclap, stop what you're doing and run for cover... You too, golfers. Drop your Callaways. Metal + lightning = bad.

64. The advice to go under a tree and crouch down on the balls of your feet is one of the worst ideas ever. Lightning can make trees explode, so keep running towards the nearest shed, house, or building. A car with a sturdy metal roof can do in a pinch. Steer clear of your convertible and golf cart. And drop your clubs already.

65. Well, actually... According to the National Oceanic and Atmospheric Administration (NOAA), touching someone that just sustained a lightning injury will not shock you. Human bodies can't store electricity. Many died because of this myth. If someone ever gets struck in front of you, get them to shelter, apply first-aid, and call 911 immediately.

66. People struck by lightning get tattoo-like scars known as Lichtenberg figures... Please resist the urge to run outside wearing chainmail next time you hear a thunderclap. Sure, it looks cool, but it's not worth it.

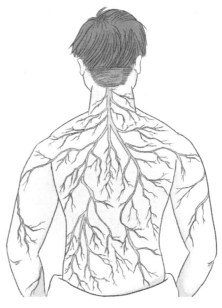

67. This or that? Lightning versus thunder. Lightning is an electrical discharge that emits light and heat. Thunder is the sound created when lightning passes through a cloud, typically a cumulonimbus cloud. Lightning superheats the air in the cloud, causing a sudden expansion. Immediately after, the air quickly cools down and violently contracts, causing the deafening sound of a thunderclap as a result. The mechanism is not too different from you blowing into an empty bag of chips and popping it. There's an expansion, a contraction, then a sound.

68. Lightning is 5 times hotter than the surface of the sun. A single bolt can reach a searing 54,000°F (30,000°C).

69. Clouds are heavy; the average cumulus cloud can weigh 1.1 million pounds (5 tonnes). Despite their density, you can't walk on clouds because they're made of water.

70. These million-pound clouds are able to float because of three main reasons. One: They're made of tiny water molecules that are lighter than the air around them. Two: They're supported by a constant flow of warm air pushing them up. And three: They absorb sunlight and heat better than air, so the droplets spread out and rise faster.

71. A nimbostratus is an evenly shaped cloud that continuously precipitates, meaning it rains, snows, and hails but doesn't emit lightning... Unfortunately, you can't hop on a nimbus and fly around the world collecting magical wish-granting orbs, even if you're pure of heart.

72. Raindrops fall at 5-20 miles per hour (8-32 kilometers per hour). It takes 1-2 minutes for rain to reach the ground.

73. Well, actually... Raindrops don't fall in a teardrop shape. Their form depends on their size and how fast they fall. Air pressure pushes them up from under and warps them into various shapes. The smallest are ball-shaped or slightly oval, medium ones are jellybean-shaped, and large ones are parachute-shaped.

74. The scent of rain is called "petrichor." When raindrops hit plants, soil, and bacteria on the ground, they burst and release the scent-causing particle geosmin.

75. Rain doesn't always make the ground wet. In hot and dry locations, like a desert road, falling rain will evaporate before it hits the pavement, leaving it as dry as a bone. This is known as "phantom rain."

76. If you get caught in the rain without an umbrella, you'll get less wet by running. Episode 1 of *Mythbusters* initially concluded that walking was better, but after more careful examination and tweaking the experiment in episode 38, they concluded that running would indeed leave you drier.

77. Blood rain is a phenomenon in which rain is dyed red. Until the 17th century, people thought it was literally raining blood —insert clever Slayer joke here. It was discovered that airborne algae spores were reacting with the raindrops as they fell. Similar types of microalgae can make rain black.

78. It's disturbingly common for it to rain fish, frogs, and even worms. Scores of little critters get swept up by tornadoes and waterspouts and are dropped far away from where they were initially. It's happened worldwide throughout the centuries, but in Yoro, Honduras, it's a yearly occurrence. Without fail, at least once between the spring and summer, fish will fall from the sky.

79. Tornadoes are indeed strong enough to lift cows into the air. There is footage of it happening in Kansas, but most famously, storm chaser Reed Timmer recorded several cows on an empty field in Cheyenne, Wyoming, being whisked away to God knows where.

80. Well, actually... A Butterfly in Brazil can't cause a tornado in Texas. Any air current its tiny wings generated would dissipate right then and there. Even if it were strong enough to cause a sizable gust of wind, there are too many barriers for it to get from point A to B undisrupted.

81. Tornadoes happen most often in the spring but can occur in the winter. They usually show up around 3:00-9:00 p.m., but they have flexible schedules.

82. Tornadoes aren't isolated to rural areas or the plains. They can hit mountain villages and densely packed cities like Chicago or Atlanta, and they can easily cross over water. You won't always see or hear them coming until it's too late.

83. Well, actually... Tornados can come from any direction, not just southwest to northeast. Opening your windows in an attempt to prevent your house from exploding will only make it easier for wind and debris to get inside. Experts recommend hiding in your basement with closed windows under a sturdy table, never inside cars or under bridges.

84. This or that? Tornadoes and hurricanes are both strong winds that flow in a spiral motion, but they are worlds apart. Tornadoes form on dry land, stop after a few hours, don't often exceed 0.5 miles (0.8 kilometers) in width, and can reach speeds of 300 miles per hour (480 kilometers per hour). Hurricanes, however, form over warm water, last up to 3 weeks or more, are several hundred times larger, and blow 200 miles per hour (320 kilometers per hour).

85. 40% of all hurricanes in the US happen in Florida.

86. Hurricanes have names so meteorologists can tell them apart and track them.

87. Hurricane Katrina and its aftermath cost the US $125-150 billion in damages.

88. Cyclones, hurricanes, and typhoons are practically the same thing, tropical storms. The difference is their origin. Cyclones are from the South Pacific and the Indian Ocean, hurricanes are from the North Atlantic and Northeast Pacific, and typhoons are from the Northwest Pacific.

89. The deepest part of the ocean is the Challenger Deep of the Mariana Trench. Its depth is about 7 miles (11 kilometers). If Mt. Everest were dropped into the Challenger Deep, its peak wouldn't be visible for another mile (1.6 kilometers).

90. There are 117 million (recognized) lakes in the world.

91. Canada has the most lakes at 879,800. A lake is a body of water at least 0.1 square kilometers or 10 hectares, about 18.5 football fields in American terms. Finland's 188,000 puddles pale in comparison to the Great White North.

92. The Amazon contains 70% of all freshwater on Earth. Russia comes in second with about 20%, and the remaining 10% is distributed throughout the rest of the world... If there is ever a worldwide water shortage, you now know where to go.

93. Well, actually... Not all lakes are freshwater; some are saltwater. A lake becomes salty when there's a lack of fresh water flowing in, and the existing water can't drain out. The pooled water evaporates, but the salt remains.

94. The Dead Sea of Israel is a lake... "Dead Lake" isn't as romantic because it conjures up images of a murky, polluted lake littered with three-eyed fish that have gone belly up.

95. The Dead Sea has a salt concentration of 30%. It's up to 10 times saltier than ocean water. It's "dead" because nothing, save for some hardy bacteria, can thrive in such a saline environment.

96. The saltiest body of water on Earth is the Don Juan Pond of Antarctica. It has an insane saline concentration of 44%. This 4-inch (10 centimeters) deep puddle never freezes.

97. The high salt concentration of the Dead Sea lets you effortlessly float without barely moving a flipper. Don't get in your eyes, though, because it can blind you.

98. It's terrifying how easy it is to drown in the Dead Sea. People can trip or get tipped over by strong winds and find themselves upside down. This is a problem because the saltier the water is, the denser it is, making it harder to maneuver yourself and get your head back above water. If you start panicking while upside down, you will instinctively gasp for air and swallow the hypersaline water, causing you to suffocate and suffer toxic shock from the rush of sodium.

99. Israeli lifeguards recovered 8 water-logged bodies in 2018 alone. Most of the victims were elderly tourists, but some young people suffered the same fate.

100. The Dead Sea is the lowest point on Earth,. It's 1,378 feet (420 meters) below sea level.

Chapter 5

Hysterical History Facts

Up there with math, history was hands down the most boring class in high school. Who cares about past events about people that don't even exist anymore, right?

In this chapter, you'll see just how wrong we were. Ancient civilizations like the Vikings, pirates, Spartans, and the Aztecs were awesome. And the famous individuals who shaped modern history were more strange yet eerily similar to us than we realize.

Before we get historical, let's talk about dating. No, not with me. I'm married now. You missed your chance when you didn't ask me out to prom... Anywho, the world is becoming increasingly globalized, and historians are getting with the times by adopting a religiously-neutral form of date-keeping. So we, the sophisticated intellectuals that we are, will follow suit.

BC (Before Christ) is now BCE (Before Common Era), and AD is CE (Common Era). Some rebellious scholars use "Current Era" instead, but it's not as common. On a side note, AD doesn't mean "After Death." It's "Anno Domini," Latin for "Year of the Lord."

***

1. Every weekday except for Monday is named after a Norse god. Tuesday is named after the god of war, Tiu (Tyr), Wednesday comes from Woden (Odin), the chief Norse god, and Thursday is the day of Thor, the god of thunder. Finally, Friday is named after Frigga (Freya), the Norse goddess of love and fertility.

2. Monday is named after the Moon. Sunday, of course, is the Sun's day. Saturday belongs to Saturn, the Roman god of agriculture (aka Cronus in Greek mythology).

3. Vikings didn't write much about themselves. Most of what we know about them comes from secondhand accounts, information passed on by their victims and enemies. Now, that's metal! It's believed Vikings originated from the area around Denmark, Norway, and Sweden.

4. It's believed that to enter the wild berserker state, the Vikings would ingest mushrooms and/or drink copious amounts of mead (a fermented alcoholic honey beverage) to dull their sense of pain and cold. This concoction allowed them to rush into battle wearing bear and wolf pelts for armor and fearlessly slay all who stood before them.

5. Vikings were quite vain. They bathed once a week and often groomed themselves with combs, ear cleaners, razors, and tweezers made of animal bones and horns. They made sure to always look fabulous on the battlefield.

6. Well, actually… Vikings didn't wear helmets with horns. Many didn't wear headgear at all. The horned helmets were an artistic liberty taken by costume designer Carl Doepler for Wagner's 1876 musical *The Ring of Nibelung*.

7. Vikings weren't pirates, warriors, and slave traders year-round. Much of their time was spent farming, manufacturing goods, building boats, or traveling to other lands for trade.

8. Vikings didn't call themselves "Vikings." The origin word "vikingar" meant "raider." The term "Viking" to identify the old Norse raiders is relatively recent.

9. Pirates were surprisingly orderly. No fighting was allowed on the ship, everyone did their chores, no one ate more than the other, loot was split evenly, and their poop decks had to be clean at all times.

10. Smart swashbucklers went out of their way to not slaughter every-one aboard the ships they invaded, so long as they surrendered. They understood that if they became known as indiscriminate killers, future victims would put up a fiercer fight, leading to unnecessary problems in the long run.

11. Well, actually... Not that many pirates met their end by jumping off a plank. Most of them were quickly dispatched by way of bullet or knife, thrown overboard, or simply stranded on a deserted island.

12. One of the most terrifying pirate punishments was keelhauling, which was specially reserved for mutinous rapscallions. Back-stabbing bilge rats were tied to the ship's edge and dragged across the water. It was like waterboarding but worse because they would be scraped up by the sharp barnacles that clung to the vessel.

13. To create an intimidating aura that struck fear into the hearts of his victims and enemies, Edward Teach (aka Blackbeard) would weave hemp threads through his facial hair and light the tips on fire before making his dramatic entrance.

14. One of, if not *the*, most feared and successful pirates in history —more than Blackbeard, even— was Ching Shih, aka Madame Cheng, a Chinese lady of the night turned into the boss lady of the pirates. With thousands of ruthless men under her command, Madame Cheng ruled the Asian seas during the 19th century and was unstoppable.

15. Pirates most likely wore eye patches to become better, more versatile fighters. If they were on a ship brawling in bright sunlight and then suddenly had to move down under the deck where it was dark, they could instantly adapt to the stark contrast in lighting by switching the eye their patch covered. It takes about 20 minutes or more for the human eye to fully adjust to darkness.

16. Well, actually... Pirates didn't always bury their booty and make a treasure map where "X" marks the spot. They needed quick access to their secret stash to buy booze, get wenches, and fuel their other pirate-ly vices.

17. Pirates could make many years' worth of money from the spoils of just one captured ship. Some could expect a $1.2 million payday from at least one raid in their lifetime. Navy officers made a paltry $580 a month, so many changed careers upon seeing the opportunities of a life of crime.

18. Julius Caesar was once kidnapped and held for ransom by pirates. They demanded 20 talents ($600,000), but he wasn't having any of it. He insisted they raise his ransom to 50 talents ($1,500,000). Caesar then told them he would crucify them when set free, but they laughed at him. Upon release, the Emperor gathered a navy, found the scallywags, and made good on his promise. He got his 50 talents back, too.

19. Well, actually... Gaius Julius Caesar (his full name) wasn't born via cesarean section. The procedure existed in 100 BCE, but it was risky, given the poor sanitization and limited medical technology of the time. C-sections were used as a last resort when doctors were sure the mother wouldn't make it through childbirth. Caesar's mother, Aurelia, lived for long after his birth.

20. In preparation for war with North Africa in 46 BCE, who used elephants in battle, Caesar sent elephants to his army to get his men and the horses used to these large and intimidating creatures. Soldiers were encouraged to touch the long-noses and instructed on where to strike for max damage, and the skittish horses were made to stand by the elephants to get used to their unfamiliar smells and sounds. It worked. The cavalry was unfazed when faced with the beasts in battle.

21. More than 60 people conspired to Caesar's assassination in 44 BCE. He was stabbed 23 times by several people but received only one fatal wound to his heart. This was a cunning way of preventing any one specific culprit from being singled out.

22. Cleopatra VII and Caesar became official in 46 BCE, while he was married to his third wife, Calpurnia. What started as a mutually beneficial power move became one of the most famous affairs in history. Caesar didn't keep his extramarital relationship with the Egyptian queen under wraps and even had an illegitimate son with her, Ptolemy XV Caesar (Caesarion), who he proudly confirmed was his.

23. Well, actually... Cleopatra wasn't technically Egyptian. She was of Greek descent, born of Ptolemy I Soter, a general of Alexander the Great.

24. Cleopatra wasn't much of a looker, either. Her visage was average at best, with a masculine face and a large, crooked nose. Much of her charm came from her sultry voice, elegant demeanor, and her way with words. She was an intellectual who spoke 12 languages and was well-versed in astronomy, math, and philosophy.

25. Cleopatra really knew how to capture the hearts of men. In a ploy to woo Caesar while evading capture by her evil brother Ptolemy XIII during the Siege of Alexandria, Cleo wrapped herself in a carpet and had someone sneak her into Caesar's room. Caesar was pleasantly surprised and did not let her effort go to waste (wink wink).

26. Three years after Caesar's passing, Cleo went to Tarsus, Turkey, and set her sights on Mark Anthony. Knowing the general fancied himself the reincarnation of Dionysus, the god of wine and festivities, Cleo dressed as Aphrodite, who had a fling with Dionysus in Greek mythology. She spared no expense to dazzle Mr. Dionysus. Upon being summoned to meet him, Cleo arrived on a golden boat rowed by silver ores while being fanned by servants costumed as cupid.

27. Back in Alexandria, the lovers Mark and Cleo partied every night. They even formed a drinking club with their aristocrat friends called the "Inimitable Livers" in dedication to Dionysus. "Inimitable" means "so great it can't be imitated," by the way. It's believed that after getting sauced, Mark and Cleo would dress in civilian clothes and head downtown to play pranks on the unsuspecting people... It's mind-blowing that pranks were a thing from as far back as 41 BCE.

28. Elagabalus (aka Antoninus) served as Rome's emperor from age 14 to 18 for 4 years until he was assassinated. Elagabalus wasn't much of a ruler, but he was an original prankster. During dinner parties, he would sneak makeshift whoopie fart cushions under the seats of Roman aristocrats and lead inebriated guests into a dungeon room filled with wild beasts, where he would lock them in for a few minutes before releasing them. The animals were docile, but the poor drunks didn't know that.

29. During the Crisis of the Third Century, from 235 to 284 CE, Rome was in absolute economic and political chaos. In the span of 49 years, more than 20 emperors were slain. Emperor Aurelian ended the crisis and unified the warring states, paving the way for Diocletian to establish a proper social system. After 21 years of service, Diocletian retired and decided to spend the rest of his days gardening. Without delay, his successors threw Rome back into turmoil. When the people begged Diocletian to retake the throne, he declined, explaining that he was too busy growing vegetables. He had enough of that crap.

30. Toilet paper was invented in sixth-century China. The first western TP was only sold in 1857 and used for hemorrhoids. Joseph Gayetty marketed his hemorrhoid healing wipes as "Medicated Paper, for the Water-Closet."

31. "Water-closet" is what "W.C." stands for. The first washrooms were closets with running water at the bottom to flush out waste.

32. Toilet paper as we know it didn't exist until 1871, when Seth Wheeler had the idea of rolling toilet tissue and dividing it into easy-to-tear squares. The word "toilet paper" was too vulgar at the time, so he sold it as "perforated wrapping paper."

33. Well, actually... The right way to hang toilet rolls, as Seth the creator intended, is to drape the sheet over and in front of the roll. NOT behind and NOT under... ladies. Please see Patent #465,588 for irrefutable proof.

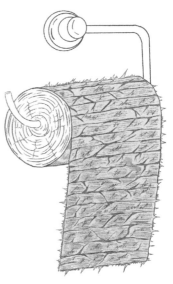

34. Splinters were a very real problem in the first bog rolls. Splinter-free toilet paper was only invented in 1935... Thank you, Northern Tissue Company!

35. Before toilet paper, ancient Romans would use a xylospongium (aka a tersorium), a wet sponge-on-a-stick, to wipe themselves clean. Public latrines came equipped with two streams of running water; one under the toilets to flush away feces and another in front to rinse the sponge with, which would be reused and shared with hundreds of other patrons. When not in use, tersoriums were kept in small water containers, soaking up each other's filth.

36. Roman public toilets weren't just disgusting; they were also dangerous. Some historical accounts state that these communal toilets exploded from time to time, most likely because of built-up methane gas igniting on a hot day.

37. Much to the dismay of bloodthirsty spectators in Rome, deaths in gladiatorial tournaments weren't always certain. Only 1 in every 5-10 fights resulted in a fatality. Whenever possible, the bout was stopped before the winner could deal a finishing blow unless the emperor or the overseer said otherwise.

38. Well, actually... The thumb-down gesture wasn't the signal to deal the killing blow. If anything, it was most likely a thumb-up that would seal a gladiator's fate.

39. Gladiators had unionized "death clubs" to which they would pay a subscription fee to ensure they received a proper burial. Unionized gladiators could expect their families to be compensated with a fair portion of their earnings should they be killed in action.

40. The rough and tough gladiators were vegetarian, not out of respect for animal rights, the environment, or whatever, but because it was cost-effective for the owners to feed their battle-slaves with barley, beans, and leaves.

41. Most gladiators were slaves, but some free men did it voluntarily. They were usually former soldiers with debts to settle, but a handful of nobles looking to test their mettle would also join the show.

42. Captive women were also forced to participate in the games during the first and second centuries. The gladiatrices (girl gladiators) were often pitted against each other but sometimes made to fight dwarves for the amusement of the patriarchal Emperor Domitian.

43. Involuntary gladiators could earn their freedom by winning 15 fights, which was rare and took forever because they only fought 3 times a year on average. Most of their time was spent training.

44. The most popular warriors were treated like royalty and had their own merchandise, much like athletes these days. Roman boys would play with clay figures modeled after their favorite gladiators, and girls would decorate their bedrooms with images of their idols. Portraits of gladiators lined the walls of many homes and public spaces as well.

45. By age 12, Spartan boys were stripped of all their belongings and sent to the wild, where they had to survive with nothing but a red cloak and their wits. They were forced to forage, hunt, and steal. If they got caught, they got flogged.

46. Most Spartans were buried in unmarked graves. The few allowed the honor of named headstones were men who fell in battle and women who died giving birth.

47. Well, actually... Spartans didn't throw their sick and weak babies off of cliffs. They abandoned their unwanted infants on hillsides. If they weren't found and adopted by a passerby, well, that's too bad, innit?

48. Spartan babies deemed worthy of living would be kept alone in a dark room at home. Their mothers were instructed to ignore their cries to erase their fear of darkness and loneliness... We call that "sleep training," now.

49. King Leonidas was about 60 years old when he spearheaded the Greek defense. The 300 best Spartans he selected were all veterans with sons to carry their legacy... Who said dads can't be cool?

50. It wasn't just the Spartans who fought the Battle of Thermopylae against King Xerxes' army. The Spartans' helots (serfs), the Thespians, Thebans, and other warriors also joined the fray. There's controversy over the total number of soldiers present in the Greek defense. It ranges from 1,500 to 8,000, which is still impressive considering the Persian army vastly outnumbered them with a force of up to 100,000 strong.

51. Leonidas and his troops lost, but future battles were won by the Greek alliance. They were victorious in the Battles of Platea and Mycale on land and won the Battle of Salamis at sea.

52. The Immortals, the Persian army's elite, consisted of about 10,000 members. The secret to their seeming immortality was that as soon as a warrior was KIA or incapacitated, another would wear the same armor and take their place.

53. Though Ephialtes of Trachis wasn't a disfigured hunchback like in *300*, he did betray the Greeks by showing the Persians a secret route that would let them flank the Greeks. He got his just desserts and was slain in Thessaly.

54. The Aztecs often waged war on neighboring tribes, not always to kill them in battle or take their land, but to capture prisoners to be sacrificed later. Up to 700 sacrifices were carried out yearly. They had a lot of gods to appease.

55. The Aztecs could use cocoa beans to pay their taxes. If they didn't have enough money or beans to pay the taxman, citizens would sell themselves or their children into slavery to work off their debt. Once everything was settled, their period of indentured servitude would end, and they would be released, allowed to resume their normal life, free from the ever-watching eye of the taxman. For a while.

56. The Aztecs were progressive at times. They were among the first civilizations to enforce mandatory education for children, allow women to own land, and give both sons and daughters the right to an inheritance from their parents.

57. Well, actually... The Mexica (Aztecs) knew about the wheel and its benefits, but their territories were surrounded by rough and uneven terrain, mountains, and lakes, so carts and animal labor weren't practical. It made more sense to carry goods manually and transport heavy loads by boat.

58. The Mexica were innovative in many ways, but in terms of military technology, they were stuck in the Stone Age. They had no way to manufacture bronze or iron. Their edged weapons were made of obsidian, a volcanic rock that can be made sharper than the most advanced surgical steel. Though the material is brittle, some surgeons prefer to use obsidian scalpels because they make very precise incisions and leave minimal scarring on the patients.

59. Mexico City used to be Tenochtitlan, the Aztec capital, which was surrounded by Lake Texcoco. It wasn't ideal to build their capital on a small island that could be flooded at any time, but the Aztecs did it anyway because of a prophecy. If they were to see an eagle eating a snake while perched on a cactus, then that is where they should build the most important part of their empire. As an homage to its heritage, the Mexican flag features the fabled eagle.

60. Hernán Cortés and his merry band of conquistadors weren't the only ones to blame for destroying Montezuma's empire in 1520 by trapping everyone inside the Aztec capital. Many enemy tribes like the Texcoco, who were tired of being under the Aztecs' thumb, also contributed to their downfall. More than war, it was smallpox that claimed the most lives.

61. By the time Columbus set sail for the New World in 1492, he and most Europeans already knew the Earth was round and that they wouldn't fall off it should they reach its non-existent edge. The Greeks confirmed it around 500 BCE.

62. Well, actually... Christopher Columbus never discovered America. He didn't even set foot on it. The first European to "discover" North America was the Norse explorer (Viking) Leif Erikson around 1000 CE.

63. Despite having no connection to the landmass that became the United States, early Americans began celebrating Cristoforo Colombo, instead of the other Italian explorer Giovanni Caboto (John Cabot), as a middle finger to England. There are many reasons why Columbus Day still exists, but mainly it's because Italian-Americans and government officials like having an extra holiday. That and it's a hassle to repeal national holidays. Imagine the backlash. Indigenous people probably wouldn't mind, though.

64. What Colombo did stumble across was the Bahamas and Hispaniola, the island Haiti and the Dominican Republic share. There he ruled as a tyrant, committing unspeakable atrocities against the natives and snuffing out all colonists who opposed him. The monarchy caught wind and dragged him back to Spain in chains in 1500. King Ferdinand soon released him and sent him on his merry way with a fat purse to South and Central America in 1502 for his final voyage.

65. When Columbus returned to Spain, King Ferdinand and Queen Isabella denied him further payment. While this was inconvenient, he was by no means left poor. He lived a comfortable life, and his accomplishments that paved the way for future travelers and traders were recognized... Karma doesn't always pay back, folks.

66. After he passed away in 1506, Columbus' family sued King Ferdinand and Queen Isabella. After a 20-year-long legal battle, they won and shook the crown down for gold coins, property, and other riches... Who knew you could sue the monarchy?

67. Well, actually... The first American Thanksgiving feast wasn't held in 1621 at Plymouth. A dinner already took place earlier in 1565 at St. Augustine, Florida, hosted by the Spaniard Pedro Menéndez de Avilé, who invited the Timucua natives to sit down and eat with his crew.

68. Poultry-obsessed historians debate over why we call a turkey a "turkey." It's established that Turkish merchants sold the Guinea fowl to Europeans, which they called a "Turkey cock," and soon shortened it to "turkey," but from there, things get complicated. One theory is that when English settlers came to America, they called the first big bird they came across a turkey, despite it being a completely different species. Yet the name stuck. The other theory is that when Spanish conquistadors went to the US, they brought the big bird back to Europe and passed it off as a Guinea fowl, tricking consumers into thinking the gobble-bird was a turkey cock. The truth of the turkey is murky.

69. Thanksgiving was originally a time of fasting for the Separatists, which is what the Pilgrims called themselves. They were suffering from a famine, so an exception had to be made or they wouldn't be alive to celebrate next year.

70. It's uncertain if turkey was in the feast of Plymouth, but lobster, swan, seal, and deer were on the menu. There was no cranberry sauce or pumpkin pie, though.

71. Thomas Jefferson almost canceled Thanksgiving forever. He believed that church and state should be kept separate and that blurring the line would be detrimental.

72. Thomas Jefferson loved Jesus and the Bible so much that he wrote his own version, *The Jefferson Bible: The Life and Morals of Jesus of Nazareth*. Jefferson removed all mention of miracles, focusing solely on what he gleaned from Jesus' teachings and accomplishments as a mortal.

73. If not for Sarah Josepha Hale, American Thanksgiving as we know it would've been gone forever. She argued that making Thanksgiving a national holiday would bring peace and unity during the Civil War. After persistently sending letters to every politician she could for 36 years, it was finally read in 1863 by Abraham Lincoln, who agreed and made it official.

74. Though its authorship is contested, Sarah J. Hale was most likely the true author of *Mary Had a Little Lamb*.

75. Before becoming the 16th US president, Abraham Lincoln was an accomplished lawyer and a pro-level wrestler. It's said he fought in 300 matches and only lost once. His large stature and brutal power were something to be feared and respected. He, as well as Theodore Roosevelt, were inducted into the National Wrestling Hall of Fame.

76. Abraham Lincoln is the tallest US president in history at 6 feet 4 inches (193 centimeters). James Madison of 5 feet 4 inches (163 centimeters) is the shortest.

77. Lyndon Baines Johnson would order custom-made trousers with extra room in the crotch because he claimed he had a sizeable Johnson, which he affectionately named "Jumbo." Without hesitation, LBJ would set Jumbo free whenever the chance presented itself, even at official parties.

78. If nature called in the middle of a conversation, LBJ dragged his associates into the bathroom and forced them to continue the chat while he was on the can. On another occasion, he marked his territory on a Secret Service worker. His reply to the serviceman's horrified expression, "That's all right, son. It's my prerogative."

79. Lyndon B. Johnson went out of his way to ensure every member of his family had his initials. His wife was Lady Bird Johnson, and his daughters were Lynda Bird and Luci Baines. His dog? Little Beagle Johnson... Of course.

80. JFK had one leg that was shorter than the other. Because of his naturally slanted body, he often had back pain and digestive issues. He was obsessed with his weight and brought a scale everywhere.

81. JFK was a huge James Bond fanboy, so much so that he wrote a fanfiction starring himself and his family. In his own story, he was assassinated in front of his wife and the Secret Service... I wonder what was going through his head when it happened to him in real life. Oh. Never mind.

82. President John Fitzgerald Kennedy was a Navy lieutenant in WWII. After getting hit by a Japanese destroyer, he and his crew got stranded. With no other way of communicating discreetly, Lt. Kennedy engraved a message onto a coconut, explaining that they survived and needed a boat, then had an island native deliver it to home base. He encased the life-saving coconut and used it as a paperweight during his time in the Oval Office.

83. Before JFK banned trade between the US and Cuba as a ploy to weaken the Cuban economy, JFK had his aide, Pierre Salinger, buy him cigars. As soon as he got word that 1,200 cigarros had been secured, JFK signed the papers for the embargo, making Cuban imports illegal in the US. His tobacco of choice was the H. Upmann Petit Upmann, which is no longer in production.

84. At one point in history, Fidel Castro was lauded as a hero of American values for overthrowing Fulgencio Batista's authoritarian regime in 1959. He was even a special guest on The Tonight Show back when Jack Paar was the host.

85. Fidel Castro never shaved his beard for two reasons. One: To him, removing his beard would be the same as disgracing the legacy he built. And two: He estimated that if he saved himself the 15 minutes of shaving every day for a year, he could have the equivalent of an additional ten 8-hour workdays to pursue more worthwhile endeavors... whatever those might be for a communist dictator.

86. Fidel Castro smoked his signature cigarros since he was 15 years old, but by 59, he stopped puffing on Cohibas to promote a smoke-free Cuba and lead by example. El Comandante's new stance on tobacco was, "The best thing you can do with this box of cigars is give them to your enemy." How inspiring.

87. The CIA tried its darndest to take out Castro. They gave him a box of poison-laced cigars, exploding cigars, and once sent his former lover after him to spike his drink with botulism pills. When that failed, they tried infecting him while scuba diving by switching his gear with a wetsuit contaminated with a flesh-eating fungus and a breathing apparatus infected with tuberculosis. The best one is when they hid a bomb under a pretty little seashell, hoping the dictator would notice it and pick it up like a curious child and it would detonate in his face.

88. Castro died of natural causes at the ripe old age of 90 on November 5, 2016. Curiously, thousands of Cuban and Cuban-American residents actually mourned the death of this man considered by many to have been a tyrant... I'm not sure what to make of this, either.

89. The dress Marilyn Monroe wore when she sang *Happy Birthday, Mr. President* to JFK sold for $4.8 million. The Ripley's Believe It or Not franchise bought it.

90. Well, actually... Marilyn Monroe and JFK didn't have an affair. Hearsay and a single photo of them in the same place at the same time isn't conclusive evidence... After *Happy Birthday, Mr. President*, JFK probably wouldn't have been opposed to it, though.

91. Despite her superstar status, Monroe's net worth would've been just $10 million in today's currency, peanuts compared to many A-list actors these days. Her biggest paycheck was a $1 million contract with 20th Century Fox, but in a cruel twist of fate, she passed away before she could collect it. DOD: August 4, 1962.

92. Monroe was quite fond of raw eggs. For breakfast, she would blend 2 raw eggs with warm milk —Rocky would be proud. Her usual lunch and dinner were less exotic, with a boiled lamb chop or steak with raw carrots on the side.

93. The blonde bombshell was discovered while working at a factory. A First Motion Picture Unit photographer visiting The Radioplane aircraft company found Monroe and soon introduced her to the film industry.

94. Marilyn Monroe's real name was "Norma Jeane Dougherty." "Marilyn" was given to her by Ben Lyon, then the head of Fox's casting, and she borrowed "Monroe" from her grandmother's surname. She legally changed it in 1956.

95. Colonel Sanders' first restaurant was a gas station diner in Corbin, Kentucky in 1930. He didn't serve fried chicken because it took too long to cook, opting instead for steak and country ham. By 1939, he developed a time-efficient method using a pressure cooker, and eventually opened his first Kentucky Fried Chicken in 1952 in Salt Lake City, Utah.

96. Col. Sanders worked a bucketful of other jobs in his younger years. He once served as a lawyer in Arkansas, but his career was cut short after he got into a fistfight with his own client in the middle of court. After that, he was a steamboat pilot, then took to door-to-door sales of car tires and life insurance. Most bizarrely, he delivered babies in Corbin, where families couldn't afford the luxury of a doctor.

97. Harland Sanders was still poor by age 65. In a bid to drastically change his life, he took to the streets in search of investors. He sold his brand in 1964, and it was acquired by the Heublein corporation in 1971. Despite collecting sizable royalties as the face of the company, the Colonel openly criticized the new KFC, calling the gravy slop and claiming it bastardized his dear chicken. The colonel was also known for swearing like a sailor.

98. Sanders filed a $122 million lawsuit against KFC after they prevented him from using his own recipe of 11 secret herbs and spices and opening an independent restaurant, "The Colonel's Lady's Dinner House," with his wife. Fortunately, the parties eventually settled their differences. Sanders got $1 million and renamed his new chicken shack the "Claudia Sanders Dinner House," which still stands to this day.

99. Harland Sanders was indeed a colonel, but not in the military sense. He was granted the honorary title by Kentucky Governor Ruby Laffoon because his chicken was that good. Col. Sanders initially wore a long black coat but soon switched to a white suit to hide the flour stains from breading chicken. He later dyed his beard white to complete the look.

100. Despite the fairy tales, Johnny Appleseed the person was 100% real, except his birth name was John Chapman. Mr. Chapman single-handedly spread his seed —not like that, guys— by planting apple trees throughout Illinois, Indiana, Ohio, and West Virginia from the late 1700s to early 1800s.

101. It's a well-known fact that books with more reviews do better on the market. Sadly, only 1 out of every 100 readers —just 1%— leave reviews, even if they love the book.

If you're enjoying this book so far and would like to see more like it, please consider taking a few quick seconds to write a brief review on Amazon, even if it's just a few sentences. It won't take long. Trust me, all I do is spit facts. And you already read 580 of them.

Please go to Amazon to leave your review or scan the QR code below:

Momoko and I love hearing from our readers, and we personally read every single review. Thank you! Arigatou!

Chapter 6

Fascinating Facts from Around the World

Do you ever wish you had all the time and money in the world and zero responsibilities? What if you could spend the rest of your life visiting every country, making friends around the globe, and experiencing every wonder the world offers?

Now, wouldn't that be nice? You probably won't be able to live out that dream to its fullest —feel free to prove me wrong— but you can still fulfill part of it. It's doable and totally worth it, even if it's just for two weeks a year. If you are one of the lucky few blessed with the means to go anywhere at any time, go to hell... and send me a postcard... and bring souvenirs. I'm getting a bit homesick.

Whether you're an eternal globetrotter or an infrequent flyer, you will have a blast discovering the unique quirks and traditions of Mexico, Hawaii, Denmark, and many other fascinating countries in this chapter.

You'll also learn surprising language facts and what not to do when traveling abroad. If you don't follow certain cultural rules, you will embarrass yourself and make the locals think you're just another stupid tourist. Worse yet, if you don't read up on the often obscure and insane laws that some countries have, you could get in big trouble for breaking them, even if you did it by accident. "I didn't know" won't always fly.

***

1. The official bird of Madison, Wisconsin, is the plastic flamingo, a literal piece of plastic molded in the shape of the lanky, pink bird. It became Madison's "bird" in 2009 because Doug Moe, a newspaper columnist, suggested it to the city council. The board thought it was quite humorous indeed and allowed it. Moe was inspired by a prank from 1979 when Wisconsin University students decorated the lawn near the dean's office with exactly 1,008 plastic pink flamingos.

2. You can technically go to jail for eating fried chicken with a fork in Gainesville, Georgia. A woman actually got locked up for breaking this law but was released soon after.

3. The fine for detonating a nuclear bomb in Chico, California, is just $500... It's good to know they don't let crimes go unpunished over there.

4. If you plan to commit a crime in the state of Texas, you are mandated by law to give the police 24 hours' advance notice, either verbally or on paper. Failure to notify the authorities will land you in jail.

5. It's illegal to sell toothpaste and a toothbrush at the same time on a Sunday in Providence, Rhode Island.

6. It's illegal to tell your customers you're a thespian in Los Angeles. Actors working as waiters on the side must keep their secret identity a secret.

7. It's a criminal offense to polish your wood while naked in Devon, Texas. You simply can't buff a table in the buff... A lot of Texans must have been doing it if an actual law had to be made to stop it.

8. It's unlawful to tie a dollar bill on a string, leave it on the ground, and pull on it to make people chase it in Pennsylvania... How much of a problem was this?

9. The technical term for dotting your i's and crossing your t's is tittling and crossbarring. Tittles are also used in lower case j's, while crossbars are also present in lowercase e's, f's, and upper case A's and H's.

10. A single sentence containing all 26 letters of the English alphabet is called a "pangram." An example of a pangram is "the quick brown fox jumps over the lazy dog."

11. English isn't the official language of the United States. And neither is Spanish. The US never decided on one.

12. Well, actually... The last letter of the alphabet isn't Z; it's J. J, the 26th letter, was a few centuries late to the party... J for "jerk," am I right?

13. The Hawaiian language has only 13 letters, the 5 vowels, A-E-I-O-U, 7 consonants, H-K-L-M-N-P-W, and the okina, a sort of backwards apostrophe that counts as a letter. Hawaii is also written as "Hawai'i," and read with a pause. It's called a "glottal stop."

14. Well, actually... "Aloha" doesn't just mean "hello" and "goodbye" in Hawaiian; it's literally a way of life. The spirit of aloha represents peace, love, connection to life, and spirituality... And yes, "ohana" does indeed mean "family."

15. Hawaii is the only US state that celebrates a monarch. June 11 is King Kamehameha Day... Sadly, he couldn't fire energy beams from his hands like Goku. By the way, "Kamehameha" means "turtle destruction wave" in Japanese.

16. Those Hawaiian hula flower necklaces are called "lei." If someone tries to put a lei on you, don't refuse or take it off later in their presence because that would be like spitting in their face. Pregnant women are the exception and are allowed to refuse a lei if they'd prefer. Once the festivities are done, and it's time to say aloha (goodbye), removing the lei is okay. Return it to nature by placing it on the ground, burying it, or hanging it on a tree, never in the trash.

17. Mothers-to-be may receive an open U-shaped lei if they would like one. It must be open because in Hawaiian culture, putting a closed circular lei on an expecting mother is akin to wishing her fetus' umbilical cord would wrap around its neck... Well, isn't that just peachy?

18. Pay attention to which ear you put your flower on in Hawaii, ladies. If it's on your right, it signals that you're single. If it's on your left ear, you're conveying that you and your ring finger are already spoken for.

19. Billboards are illegal in Hawaii because they take away from the gorgeous scenery. It's the same in Alaska, Maine, and Vermont.

20. The current American flag with 50 stars was designed by a high schooler named Robert Heft for a school project in 1958. He initially got a B-, but after submitting it to the White House and President Eisenhower declaring it the new official flag, his teacher bumped his grade up to an A... The kid's design became the flag of the country, yet he only got an A, not an A+. Talk about a demanding teacher.

21. The USA has 50 states, including Hawaii and Alaska. As for Puerto Rico and Washington D.C., Puerto Rico is a commonwealth, a territory, and Washington District of Columbia is, well, a district.

22. People born in Puerto Rico are technically US citizens. Oddly enough, they can't vote in presidential elections but can somehow run for president. It's a long story.

23. The bay glows bright blue at night in Puerto Rico. This is thanks to an incredible number of dinoflagellates, a type of algae that emit their own natural light. Put kayaking at night in the Fajardo Bioluminescent Bay, La Parguera, and especially Mosquito Bay on your bucket list! The view is totally worth losing a few drops of blood over.

24. The legal age to buy alcohol in Cuba is 16. That's not the worst of it, though, because there is no age requirement to drink alcohol or buy and smoke cigars.

25. The average Cuban lives on $30 a month yet has a life expectancy of about 80 years, which is comparable to developed countries. Healthcare is free in Cuba, a communist dictatorship, but not in the United States.

26. Cuba is a paradise for lovers of classic cars. Because of its political climate, few new cars are brought into Cuba. When visiting the Cuban Republic, expect to see vintage Cadillacs, Chryslers, Jaguars, and Oldsmobiles rolling on the streets. You can't bring them back home to add to your car collection, but at least you can ride them as taxis.

27. Compared to other cultures, Cubans may come off as aggressive. But don't freak out. It's normal for them to speak loudly, wave their hands about, nod and shake their heads often, and really get into your personal space. This sort of interaction is usually a sign of respect and closeness. They don't like prolonged eye contact, though.

28. Cubans also talk with their faces. If you see a Cuban puckering their lips, it's probably not to kiss you. It's how they point to something or someone without using their finger. If they wrinkle their nose, it could either be because they smelled that silent but deadly fart you let out, and they know it's you, or, hopefully, they're just asking you a question, a sort of non-verbal "Huh?" or "What?"

29. There's almost no crime in Cuba. It's one of the safest places for a globe-trotting señorita to do some solo soul searching.

30. It's a crime in Singapore to use a public toilet and forget to flush. If toilets aren't your thing, try your best not to relieve yourself in an elevator because they come equipped with sensors that detect urine and automatically shut their doors, trapping you inside until the police and possibly news reporters arrive… That's one way to get famous.

31. Connecting to your neighbors' wifi is considered a cyber hacking offense in Singapore. If your neighbor reports you, you could be looking at a $10,000 fine plus 3 years in jail, with no wifi access.

32. In Singapore, you could be fined $2,000 and jailed for 3 months for walking naked in your house. Singaporean supermodels aren't exempt from this law, unfortunately.

33. If you get caught jaywalking twice in Singapore, you'll be slapped with a $2,000 fine and 6 months of jail time. The first offense yields half the punishment.

34. It's illegal to play an instrument in a manner that annoys someone while in a public space in Singapore. The singing of obscene lyrics is also banned.

35. Don't sell or give gum in Singapore, or you could face 2 years imprisonment and fines of $100,000. The chewing of gum is also policed, but you should be fine if you have a prescription to prove it's for medical reasons, e.g., an anxiety disorder.

36. Vandalism is taken very seriously in Singapore. If you're found vandalizing property, such as painting graffiti, scratching cars with a coin, or breaking windows, you will be arrested and beaten with a stick. Two tourists were caught and caned in 2015, and another in 1994.

37. According to the Reporters without Borders survey, Singapore ranks extremely low in terms of freedom of the press. As of 2020, Singapore sits at 160 out of 180, which isn't too far off from Cuba, China, and North Korea.

38. Despite Singapore's reputation as a nanny state that puts its citizens on a short leash and its high cost of living, it's consistently rated as the top destination for ex-pats alongside Switzerland. It's very safe, very clean, the people are warm and friendly, and the food is fantastic... No, I don't have a gun to my head. I mean it.

39. The Swiss have strict noise pollution laws. It's illegal for men to pee standing up after 10:00 p.m. in Switzerland, and you can't flush the toilet until morning.

40. Switzerland takes Sundays very seriously. You can get booked for noise pollution even in the daytime on Sundays. You literally can't do everyday tasks like mowing your lawn or doing your laundry. Oh, and if you want to hand-wash all your clothes and dry them as quietly as possible, without your dryer machine, stop because you can't hang your clothes outside on a Sunday in Switzerland, either.

41. You will be charged $100 if caught hiking naked in Switzerland... $100 is a small price to pay for freedom. Who doesn't enjoy the feeling of ravenous, blood-thirsty bugs aggressively nipping at their bits?!

42. If you own social animals like dogs, guinea pigs, and goldfish, you're obligated by Swiss law to always have at least two. Suppose pet A is older and pet B is younger. If pet A dies, you must buy a new pet, C, to keep your aging pet, B, company. Then, if pet B expires, you would need to get poor pet C a new companion. There are services in Switzerland that let you rent temporary pets... I just thought I'd share this extra morsel of information, but people in Peru eat barbecued guinea pigs. It's called "cuy." The Spektor strikes again!

43. Switzerland has no capital city. Bern is the center of the Swiss federal government, but that's it. Geneva and Zurich aren't the capital, either.

44. Switzerland has four national languages, French, German, Italian, and Romansch. If you think that's impressive, Zimbabwe has 16, the most out of all countries. India is technically the most multilingual country in the world, being home to more than 19,500 languages and dialects, but they're only spoken on a small regional scale, not on a large national scale like those in Zimbabwe.

45. Switzerland and the Vatican are the only countries with square flags. Nepal gave the finger to quadrilaterals and made its flag a pair of triangles.

46. Vatican City is the smallest country in the world, measuring a diminutive 44 hectares. You could fit 8 Vaticans inside New York's Central Park.

47. Toblerone is based on Matterhorn, a mountain in the Swiss-Italian Alps. FYI, the right way to eat the triangular chocolate is to push the end piece in, not pull it apart.

48. €3,000 ($3,500) are thrown into the Trevi Fountain of Rome every day. Just in the year 2016, €1.4 million ($1.5 million) worth of coins was scooped up and used to combat poverty. The legend that inspires this spontaneous generosity states that if you throw a coin with your right hand over your left shoulder, you'll be able to visit Rome again. And if you throw 2 more coins in the same fashion, you'll find true love in Rome and have a glamorous wedding.

49. To "have your eyes covered with ham" in Italian roughly means to not see the most obvious of things for what they are. "Avere gli occhi foderati di prosciutto."

50. It's no exaggeration to say that Italian men are very attached to their mothers. According to Italy's national statistics agency, Istat, more than 50% of men aged 24-35 still live with mamma. The Catholic church blames these mammoni for the decline of marriages in Italy... "'Mammoni?!' Is that a Jojo reference?!"

51. You're legally obligated to smile at all times in Milan, Italy. The few exceptions are during hospital visits and funerals.

52. Not walking your dog at least 3 times a day is considered animal abuse in Turin, Italy. So is dying their fur.

53. It's illegal to wear flip-flops in Capri, Italy. This law extends to other noisy footwear like wooden clogs and squeaky shoes.

54. Saving a spot on the beach with a towel is strictly forbidden in Italy. Tourists were leaving their towels and other junk out on the beach overnight to hold their spot for the following morning, so something had to be done about it.

55. It's illegal to build sandcastles in Eraclea, Italy. They're deemed an obstruction on the beach and a tripping hazard much too dangerous for its delicate, egg-like citizens.

56. This or that? The Italian and Mexican flags look almost identical with their three vertical stripes of green, white, and red, so it can get confusing. The easiest way to tell them apart is to look at the middle. Mexico's flag features the fabled Aztec eagle on a cactus, while Italy's is left blank.

57. Mexico City and Venice, Italy, are sinking at an alarming rate. Some estimates indicate that the cities could be completely flooded within the next 100-150 years if nothing is done to efficiently drain the water and keep it out.

58. Statistically, Mexicans are the hardest-working people in the world. More so than even Americans, Japanese, or South Koreans. Mexicans work an average of 2,148+ hours a year.

59. Resident artists in Mexico can sell art to pay their tax bills.

60. Well, actually... Cinco de Mayo isn't Mexican independence day. Their independence day is on September 16. The 5th of May is important because it represents the day in 1862 when poorly trained Mexican soldiers managed to beat Napoleon III and his elite French forces in a battle against all odds.

61. Every year, on the eve of Mexican Independence Day, citizens gather at the town square to watch their president reenact the famous Grito de Dolores speech of Miguel Hidalgo, the priest who sparked the war of independence. In response to El Grito, they shout "¡Viva México!" ("Long live Mexico!") and go on to celebrate their victory over the Spanish with food, fireworks, and other festivities.

62. Though Día de Los Muertos is celebrated November 1-2, right after October 31, and involves lots of skulls and sugar, it's not just a Mexican Halloween. Day of the Dead isn't about dressing up and collecting candy at strangers' doors. It's to pay respects to the dearly departed, give the grim reaper a cheeky grin, and celebrate life to spite him. Colorful shrines (ofrendas) are built to honor lost loved ones. Ofrendas are decorated with flowers and then garnished with their favorite foods and drinks, where their picture sits atop. Some natives will even have a nighttime picnic next to their family graves.

63. Mexican children don't get Christmas presents. Their gifts are given to them on January 6, on Día de Los Reyes (Day of the Kings), the day the Three Wise Men are said to have visited baby Jesus. 80% of Mexicans are catholic.

64. Instead of the tooth fairy, sleeping Spanish children are "visited" by Ratoncito Pérez, a business savvy mouse that sneaks under children's pillows and trades his coins for their teeth.

65. "Pasta" means "money" in Spanish. It's like how we call money "dough." The Spanish just go a few extra steps in the cooking process.

66. A siesta is what the Spanish call a power nap. It's usually 30 minutes long, but the time window is of several hours. Spanish cities go quiet from From 2:00 p.m. to 5:00 p.m. Restaurants remain open, but shops and offices close their doors, and children playing on the street are brought inside. Many adults work through it, though. There's been talk about cutting out siestas entirely so everyone can go home earlier.

67. The oldest operating restaurant in the world is in Madrid, Spain. Restaurante Sobrino de Botín has been filling bellies with roast piglets and other Spanish delicacies since 1725 and is still going strong. Its fire oven has been burning non-stop day and night for nearly 300 years!

68 Second to Chinese (Mandarin), Spanish is the most spoken language. There are an estimated 440+ million hispanophones globally. The most Spanish speakers are not in Spain but in Mexico.

69. The Spanish national anthem doesn't have any lyrics. It's instru mental... It's easy marks in Spanish class because all you need to do is hum along or stand in silence.

70. Spain has no laws against public nudity. If you have the body positivity for it, you can rock your birthday suit and traumatize children and the elderly on the streets unchallenged. Just don't expect cake shops, or any shop in general, to let you in.

71. It's customary in Spain to eat 12 grapes to welcome the New Year. If you eat each grape in time with the 12 chimes of the clock bell, you'll have good luck that year.

72. Cambodian people celebrate New Year in April, from the 13th to the 15th. Thanks to the Khmer calendar (we use the Gregorian calendar) and Buddhism, Cambodia has the most civic holidays of all countries, with 28 days off in total.

73. Cambodia has the highest concentration of Buddhists at 95-97% percent. And the world's largest religious monument is the Angkor Wat, a huge Hindu-turned-Buddhist temple spanning 402 acres, 17.5 million square feet (or 1.6 million square meters).

74. Most Cambodian don't celebrate birthdays. The children don't care for it, and some elderly have no idea what their day of birth is; they only know the year or season they came into existence.

75. A third of the Cambodian population is less than 15 years old. During the tyrannical Khmer Rouge regime that lasted from 1975 to 1979, many citizens over the age of 50 and children and infants were executed.

76. Cambodian funerals generally last 3-7 days. The loved one's body is washed, dressed, kept at home for several days, then cremated on the last. These funerals are extravagant affairs costing $9,000, a shocking amount considering the average monthly salary in Cambodia is about $100. Family members pour out their life savings and sell their most valuable possessions to pay for the ceremony.

77. Cambodia, Thailand, and Taiwan are the top 3 most LGBTQ-friend-ly countries. Many Cambodians believe their King Norodom Sihamoni is gay himself... "Themself?" Sorry folks, I'm still getting used to the new personal pronouns. I try to be inclusive.

78. The Netherlands was the first country in history to legalize same-sex marriage, back in 2001. Since then, more than 15,000 homosexual couples got hitched.

79. Amsterdam is world-famous for its coffee shops that let its patrons legally smoke cannabis and hash. No more than 5 grams of product may be sold per transaction, though. Many Dutch people never touched the stuff.

80. Well, actually... The majority of Dutch people don't own wooden clogs, and some have never even worn them. A handful of farmers use clogs, but they're sold mainly as souvenirs for tourists. Up to six million klompen are made every year.

81. The Dutch are the tallest people in the world. The average height is about 5-feet-9 (176 centimeters), with many men towering at 5-feet-12 (183 centimeters) tall.

82. There are more bikes than people in the Netherlands; it has 22 million bicycles to 17 million citizens. The Dutch love their bikes and ride them whenever possible, cycling an average of 1.85 miles (3 kilometers) daily. Except for the over 100,000 bicycle thefts every year, the Netherlands is an excellent country for cyclists.

83. Of all the countries where English is not a native language, the Dutch score highest on the worldwide EF English Proficiency Index. 90-93% of the population is fluent in English, which means you could get by in the Netherlands and have a great time traveling there without knowing a lick of Dutch. You should if you plan to live there and get citizenship.

84. By Danish tradition, if you're unmarried by age 25, your friends and family get to tie you up and throw cinnamon powder at you on your birthday. If you're still single at 30, you get pelted with pepper. To rub more pepper into the wound, your cheeky friends may also give you a peppermill. Chronically single Danish women are pebermo ("pepper lasses"), and the men are pebersvend ("pepper lads").

85. It's customary in Danish weddings for the groomsmen to lift the groom up in the air, take off his shoes, and cut the tips of his socks. It's believed that this sock circumcision originated as a way to make men faithful. In the olden days, some men would take off their wooden clogs to pay their mistress a late-night visit without being heard. Returning with dirty socks would signal their dishonesty. The other theory is that this sock-cutting tradition serves to give the bride her first task as a wife, to mend her husband's socks. Most Danish husbands these days are progressive enough just buy new socks themselves.

86. If the groom leaves the room during the party, even briefly, Danish tradition demands that the groomsmen line up to kiss the bride. Equally, if the bride steps out, the bridesmaids kiss the groom.

87. The Danish flag (aka the Dannebrog) is the oldest flag in the world that is still in use. This red flag with a white cross has remained unchanged since 1219.

88. Danish summers reach an average temperature of just 60°F (16°C), but that doesn't stop people from surfing in its frigid waters. One of the best surfing spots in the world is a place in Denmark called "Cold Hawaii."

89. Every Summer, scores of Santa Clauses from around the world come to the World Santa Claus Congress in Denmark to drink, sing, and bathe together in the hot springs of the Bakken Amusement Park. By the way, the Bakken has been running since 1583, making it the oldest amusement park in history.

90. Lego building blocks were invented in Denmark in 1958 by Ole Kirk Christiansen. The name is a combination of "leg" and "godt," which means "play well" in Danish.

91. It's illegal to advertise to children under 12 in Norway. No commercials about action figures, dolls, or sugary cereals are shown.

92. There's no life sentence in Norway, and there hasn't been since 1971. The maximum is 21 years, in most cases. The reconviction rate is 20%.

93. Norway was crowned the happiest place on Earth in 2017. It also reigned supreme in the Human Development Index, which analyzes GDP, education, and life expectancy, for 9 years between 2001 and 2011, excluding 2007 and 2008.

94. Despite being the king of Norway, the late Olav V (the fifth) didn't drive a car or use a personal chauffeur. He used public transportation and insisted that he paid for his ride. Olav V was very much liked by the Norwegian people.

95. In Northern Norway, the Sun never sets in the summer, and it never rises in the winter. These events are the Midnight Sun and the Polar Night, respectively... Dude, that's so power metal!

96. There's a small Norwegian town called "Hell," and it freezes over every winter.

97. The world's highest ATM is also at Khunjerab Pass. Even surrounded by snow at 15,400 feet (4,700 meters) high, it's fully operational and regularly loaded with cash.

98. The highest highway on Earth is the Karakoram Highway, located at Khunjerab Pass, between the China-Pakistan border. Trucks and cars can be seen driving at the highway's peak of 15,465 feet (4,715 meters).

99. Pakistan is the first Islamic country to have a female prime minister. Benazir Bhutto led Pakistan from 1988 to 1990 and from 1993 to 1996.

100. There's a special police force in Karachi, Pakistan, in which they chase after criminals while wearing rollerblades and holding guns... Let's hope the bad guys never find out they can just run on the sand. Karachi has lots of beaches.

Chapter 7

Entertaining Pop Culture Facts

There are too many things to write about for pop culture. There's enough to make a book series about it. I'm a millennial, so this chapter focuses on things millennials like myself might find nostalgic. I wouldn't want the other generations to think I'm entitled, so I sprinkled in some stuff from other decades.

Even if you weren't born between 1981 and 1996, don't skip this chapter because you might find something you like. At the very least, you'll pick up some useful canned conversation-starters for if you're ever forced to be around a millennial.

You will learn new things about sorta old things, little-known behind-the-scenes facts about classic books, movies, music, and retro videogames, as well as some intriguing, inspiring, and idiosyncratic tidbits about authors, actors, and artists, plus the surprising origins of some of the biggest memes in internet history.

Apologies to my fellow weebs. There isn't much Japan, anime, or manga-related content in this book besides some very clever references written by yours truly. Don't worry, because I have a Japan and manga/anime factbook in the works. Check on my Bryan Spektor Amazon author page every once in a while.

Without further ado, let's get to the good stuff.

***

1. *Lilo and Stitch* started out as a children's book in 1985 titled *Lilo and Stitch, A love story of a girl and what she thinks is a dog.* It was written by Chris Sanders, the animated feature's director and the voice of Stitch.

2. The tall, dark, and intimidating Agent Cobra Bubbles was inspired by Marcellus Wallace, the *Pulp Fiction* gangster who once whacked a guy for massaging his wife's feet. Coincidentally, Ving Rhames, who played Wallace, was Bubbles' voice actor.

3. Daveigh Chase, who voiced Lilo, also played Samara, the girl from *The Ring*. Both films were released in 2002. A year prior, Chase voiced Chihiro from *Spirited Away*.

4. Ghibli has had some surprisingly high-profile talent. Gillian Anderson (Agent Scully from *The X-Files*) voiced Moro, the wolf mother from *Princess Mononoke*. Michael Keaton (*Batman Returns*) played the high-flying Porco from *Porco Rosso*. Christian Bale (*The Dark Knight*) was Howl, the hunky wizard from *Howl's Moving Castle*. And Mark Hamill, the original Luke Skywalker and the best animated Joker, was Colonel Muska, the villain in *Laputa: Castle in the Sky*.

5. The name "Ghibli" comes from an Italian WWII airplane. Miyazaki loves Italy, and he really loves planes. Ghibli (with a "G" like Gibson) is also the Arabic name of the Hot Saharan Wind. From its inception, Studio Ghibli set out to "blow new wind through the anime industry."

6. Upon their 1988 release in Japanese theatres, the heart-wrenching *Grave of the Fireflies* and the heartwarming *My Neighbor Totoro* were shown as a double-feature. *Totoro* was played second to soften the emotional blow dealt by the first movie... If you haven't watched *Grave of the Fireflies* yet, get ready to cry. A lot.

7. The city in *Kiki's Delivery Service* was an imagination of 1950s Europe if WWII didn't happen. Inspiration was taken from Italy, France, and Sweden.

8. Despite all the fame and fortune, Gayla Peevey, the singer of the 1953 smash hit *I Want a Hippopotamus For Christmas*, never got a hippopotamus for Christmas. There is no justice in this world.

9. Hip-hop overtook rock as America's music of choice in 2017... These are dark times we live in, rock fans.

10. The first rap record in history was *Rapper's Delight.* It was released in 1979 by The Sugarhill Gang. Long before rappers, though, there were Viking Skalds. Just like their contemporary counterparts, Skalds would recite verses and rhymes that often included obscenity, violence, and social commentary. They would also boast about themselves or the heroes of their generation.

11. Slim Shady's favorite book is the dictionary. As a teenager, Marshall Bruce Mathers III would read the dictionary to add new and interesting words to his vocabulary.

12. Eminem hates it when people say that nothing rhymes with "orange." During a *60 Minutes* interview with Anderson Cooper, Eminem went out of his way to make a short rap song with lyrics that rhymed 11 times with "orange."

13. The only single word that perfectly rhymes with "orange" is "sporange," which is the spore-making organ that moss, mold, and mushrooms use to reproduce asexually. "Silver" is another word thought to be unrhymable. "Chilver" rhymes with "Silver." A chilver is a female lamb. Nothing rhymes with "pint," though.

14. Elton John can confirm that, despite his lyrics, Eminem isn't a homophobe. They're actually really good friends. Sir John dedicated 18 months of his life to helping Eminem beat his drug addiction, and they even did a duet of *Stan* at the 43rd Grammy Awards. Eminem couldn't attend Elton's wedding, so he sent the grooms a very special pair of diamond-encrusted rings, the kind that doesn't go on your finger (wink wink).

15. The bully Eminem mentions in *Brain Damage*, DeAngelo Bailey, tried suing Em, claiming the song slandered his good name and violated his privacy. He lost the case after the judge delivered her verdict in rhyme: "Bailey thinks he's entitled to some monetary gain because Eminem used his name in vain. The lyrics are stories no one would take as fact, they're an exaggeration of a childish act." Savage.

16. Eminem doesn't like computers. He explained in an interview with MTV that he's afraid of getting sucked in and reading mean comments about him. The world-famous rapper considers himself an introvert.

17. Well, actually... Eminem isn't the fastest rapper out there. The Rap God can spit out 10 syllables per second, and that's impressive, but the Texan rapper Crucified can rapid-fire 20 syllables per second.

18. People who listen to Eminem are psychopaths, according to a 2017 study conducted at New York University. Fans of *Lose Yourself* scored highest on psychopathy tests. Fans of Justin Bieber, especially of *What Do You Mean?* were also noted to have abnormal brains.

19. Dr. Dre's real name is Andre Romelle Young. When he first worked as a DJ, his stage name was "Dr. J," in homage to the basketball player Julius Erving. After realizing that Dr. J the DJ lacked pizzazz, he sat down, thought long and hard, and came up with the most creative name he could think of, "Dr. Dre," inspired by his first name, Andre.

20. Puffy, Puff Daddy, P. Diddy, and Diddy, are all the same person, Sean Jean Combs, except he isn't Sean Jean Combs and he isn't Diddy. Not anymore. He changed his legal name to Sean Love Combs, and now goes by Brother Love.

21. Dr. Dre had his first child when he was 16 years old. Dre didn't meet his son until 20 years later, only after he, the son, became a rapper himself, Hooded Surgeon.

22. If it weren't for Eminem, 50 Cent would never have released *Get Rich or Die Tryin'*. Dr. Dre was hesitant to sign Fiddy to his label, so Em offered Dre a 50-50 split for the cost between their labels, Aftermath Entertainment and Shady Records, to minimize the risk. The gamble paid off, and 50 Cent's album became the best-selling album of 2003 and went multi-platinum.

23. 50 Cent did indeed get shot 9 times. If it weren't for Dr. Nader Paksima, he wouldn't have lived to tell the tale. Even though he had more than enough money by 2003 to pay for the $32,500 he owed in medical bills, Mr. Half A Dollar didn't spare a cent for the man who saved his life, so his doctor sued him.

24. Before becoming a rap star, Curtis James Jackson III was a drug dealer. What is surprising, though, is that he never got high off his own supply. Fiddy confesses that he never smokes. The song *I Get High All the Time* was just good marketing.

25. 50 also goes to great lengths to not drink alcohol, not even his own champagne, Le Chemin du Roi. When at the club, he first pours out all the champagne for his homies, then secretly fills it with ginger ale. Like a child with a teddy bear, he clutches that bottle all night, taking a sip whenever he has to look cool.

26. The oversized clock on Flavor Flav's neck isn't just a gimmick; it's a philosophy. Flav wears his absurd timepiece to remind himself and his fans that the most important thing you have is time and that you have to live every second to the fullest because you have only one short life.

27. Outkast's *Hey Ya!* is often played at weddings, which is ironic because the lyrics are about people in unhappy relationships. It talks about how people stay in a relationship because they feel they have to, rather than being true to their feelings and breaking up.

28. Well, actually... You're not supposed to shake a Polaroid picture because it damages it. Just give it a few seconds to dry on its own.

29. A pair of leather gloves almost ruined the *Skyfall* movie. During one of his breaks, Daniel Craig bought a pair of gloves and insisted he wear them in the next scene. The director, too tired of Craig's tantrums to say "no," allowed it. Big mistake. During the fight scene in the komodo dragon pit, a bad guy takes Bond's gun and tries to shoot him with it but is unable because it has a fingerprint scanner, which Bond then picks up and fires. Bond wearing gloves in that scene would've created a huge plot hole, but reshooting would cost millions, so post-production had to digitally paint Craig-colored hands over the gloves frame-by-frame.

30. Daniel Craig said he absolutely hated playing James Bond, calling 007 a misogynist, and that he would rather off himself than be Bond again. Craig reprised his role for the sequel *No Time to Die*. He's still alive and kicking.

31. Welsh actor Desmond Llewelyn holds the record for the most times an actor played the same character in a movie franchise. 17. You might know him as "Q," the Quartermaster who feeds James Bond's unhealthy gadget addiction.

32. Roger Moore, the third James Bond, was so embarrassed of the way he ran that he had a double step in for every scene in his career involving anything more intense than a power walk.

33. Sean Connery wore a toupée in every scene he did as James Bond. He had the bad luck of going bald at a young age —I can relate. Before he was a Bond, Connery was a bodybuilder. Before *that*, the shekshy bashtard was a nude model.

34. Christopher Lee was Ian Fleming's cousin. Lee was offered the leading role in the first Bond film, *Dr. No*, but he declined. Fleming hated *Dr. No* with Sean Connery, calling it "simply dreadful." A decade later, Lee made his cousin happy by starring in *The Man With the Golden Gun* as the triple-nippled psychopath Francisco Scaramanga.

35. Ian Fleming chose to call his iconic spy character "James Bond" because it was the most boring name he could think of. "James Bond" was the name of an ornithologist, a professional bird-watcher, essentially.

36. GoldenEye, the title of both the 17th James Bond movie and the Nintendo 64 game, was originally the name of Ian Fleming's house in Jamaica. Bob Marley lived there for a few months.

37. Christopher Lee was a *Lord of the Rings* fanboy long before he got a part in the movies. It's said that he read the novels every year. His dream was to play Gandalf, but Peter Jackson told him he was too old and frail to handle the fight scenes, so he was cast as the corrupted wizard Saruman. Lee reluctantly accepted.

38. Christopher Lee was the only LoTR crew member to have met J.R.R. Tolkien. They bumped into each other at a pub at Oxford University in the 1950s. Tolkien and Lee passed away in 1973 and 2015, respectively.

39. Elijah Wood got the role of Frodo Baggins by cosplaying as a hobbit and recording his audition tape in the woods.

40. Eight of the nine actors who played the fellowship (Frodo and company) got matching tattoos of the Elvish script for "Nine" to remember their time working together in the LoTR trilogy. John Rhys-Davies declined, so his stunt double, Brett Beattie, got it in his place.

41. Though he played Gimli the dwarf, John Rhys-Davies is the tallest member of the main cast. He is over 6 feet (1.8 meters) tall.

42. Andy Serkis modeled Gollum's mannerisms after drug addicts going through withdrawal. Gollum's raspy voice was inspired by cats coughing up hairballs.

43. The blood-curdling screams of the Nazgul, Sauron's demonic Black Riders, were made by rubbing cheap plastic cups together and distorting the sound. Fans once speculated it was a horse in heat.

44. The Beatles almost made a LoTR film in the 1960s starring themselves, with George Harrison as Gandalf, Paul McCartney as Frodo, Ringo Starr as Sam, and John Lennon as Gollum. Even with Stanley Kubrick at the helm, Tolkien shot down the idea without batting an eye of Sauron.

45. Tolkien and his wife Edith are buried in Oxford, England. On their tombstones are the names of two lesser-known characters, the star-crossed lovers Beren and Luthien, the tragic couple of a mortal man and an immortal elf.

46. Even after his death, John Ronald Reuel Tolkien is still making a killing. As of 2021, his novels have sold 600 million copies. The #1 best-selling fiction author is William Shakespeare, with 4 billion sales.

47. Tolkien loved trolling people. As a senior, he would mix some of his false teeth into the money he paid shopkeepers. In his younger years, Tolkien once went to a non-Halloween party dressed as a polar bear. Just for fun, he would occasionally dress up as an Anglo-Saxon warrior and chase his neighbors down the street while swinging an ax.

48. Up to a point, Tolkien and C.S. Lewis were close friends, but they gradually split after Tolkien, a devout Catholic, felt that Lewis was straying from the path and prioritizing a life of hedonism. After his death, however, Tolkien wrote a letter to Lewis' daughter, lamenting the loss of his dear friend, Clive Staples Lewis.

49. C.S. Lewis was born with monkey hands. He had one less joint at the thumb than most humans. Because of his simian digits, Lewis couldn't throw a ball or swing a bat, so he was picked on at school. The jokes on them because he became a famous writer.

50. Though his day job as an academic earned him a very modest income, Lewis donated all his royalties from *The Chronicles of Narnia* to charity. Despite his kindness, he was taxed to the hilt by the government and made to pay out of pocket... No good deed goes unpunished.

51. 3,000 actors auditioned for the role of Peter Pevensie for the films. Ultimately, Director Andrew Adamson gave the part to William Moseley. For the White Witch, though, Adamson knew he wanted Tilda Swinton to play her from the start.

52. You might be disappointed after eating real Turkish delight (lokum), the magical treat that Edmund basically sold out his own family for. Many non-Turkish people who tried this sticky mixture of sugar, water, starch, and rosewater tossed in powdered sugar describe it as sickly sweet and say it tastes like their gramma's potpourri... I've had it myself and would say that's about right.

53. The reactions of amazement by Georgie Henley (Lucy) and Skandar Keynes (Edmund) when they first entered Narnia were genuine. The director kept the actors in the dark until the big reveal.

54. C.S. Lewis, Aldous Huxley (of *Brave New World*), and President John F. Kennedy all died on the same day, November 22, 1963.

55. Inspired by this bizarre coincidence, Peter Kreeft wrote a book very aptly titled *Between Heaven and Hell: A Dialog Somewhere Beyond Death with John F. Kennedy, C. S. Lewis, & Aldous Huxley*, in which the three discuss the Christian faith while in Purgatory.

56. Arthur Conan Doyle was knighted in 1902 by King Edward VII, not for *Sherlock Holmes* but for his essay The War in South Africa: Its Cause and Conduct, which defended England's participation in the Boer war.

57. Famed escape artist Harry Houdini and Arthur Conan Doyle, the author of *Sherlock Holmes*, were friends. That is until Houdini one day learned that Sir Doyle, the guy who writes books about solving mysteries with science and logic, believed in all seriousness that Houdini had magic powers. The bromance ended right then and there.

58. 60% of British people once believed that Sherlock Holmes, the character, was real. Fans would unironically send letters to Sir Doyle, requesting his fictional character's detective services to solve their real-world problems.

59. Sir Doyle grew so tired of Sherlock Holmes that he killed him off in 1893. In *The Adventure of the Final Problem*, Holmes and his nemesis Dr. Moriarty plummeted to their deaths from atop a waterfall. The backlash from fans forced him to resurrect Holmes 10 years later in *The Adventure of the Empty House*.

60. Sir Doyle did some detective work of his own and proved the innocence of two men. George Edaji, a lawyer accused of mutilating animals, and Oscar Slater, a man falsely charged with the murder of an old woman, were liberated.

61. Sherlock Holmes revolutionized the way crime scene investigations are carried out in the real world. He popularized the forensic analysis of fingerprints, shoe prints, tire tracks, handwriting, and ballistics. Ballistics is the study of bullets and their effects upon firing.

62. Well, actually... The original Sherlock Holmes never said, "Elementary, my dear Watson." Doyle didn't coin the catchphrase. Holmes didn't wear a deerstalker cap either, as far as Doyle's concerned.

63. In summary, "discombobulate" means to confuse or disorient a person. Cupping your hands and slapping their ears real hard will most certainly discombobulate them, and also rupture their eardrums.

64. Next to Dracula, with 272 appearances and counting, Sherlock Holmes is the most portrayed literary character. The ace detective has made 254+ appearances and has been played by more than 75 actors, including Jeremy Brett, Benedict Cumberbatch, and several dogs.

65. D. H. Lawrence would climb mulberry trees naked to get his creative juices flowing. Lawrence's works include *Aaron's Rod*, *The Plumed Serpent*, and *The White Peacock*.

66. Agatha Christie, the queen of murder mystery, got her most sick and twisted ideas while soaking in a warm, cozy bath and eating sweet, fresh apples.

67. Only 15 minutes of the classic 1993 *Jurassic Park's* 2-hour run time features dinosaurs... Take note, future filmmakers. Sometimes less is more.

68. Arianna Richards got the role of Lex, the big sister in *Jurassic Park*, by screaming the loudest. Rather than read lines, Steven Spielberg asked auditioning girls to scream into a microphone. He found his Lex after Richards' recording woke his wife in the middle of the night and made her rush to their children's room to see if they were okay.

69. The scene when the *T. rex* breaks the glass sunroof of the Ford Explorer wasn't planned; the robot malfunctioned. The cries of Lex and Tim were of genuine terror because they were in actual danger.

70. One staff member was almost killed by the *T. rex*, too. Alan Scott, an animatronics tech, had to crawl into the belly of the beast to attach its artificial skin. Depending on if it was turned on or off, the machinery would engage to change the position of the robot's head. If a sudden power outage were to shut it off with him in it, the powerful hydraulic pistons and sharp metal sheets would crush and dice him like a tomato. The blackout happened, but he somehow made it out unharmed.

71. The terrifying roars of the *T. rex* were made by combining the noises of a tiger, an alligator, and a baby elephant, then slowing them down.

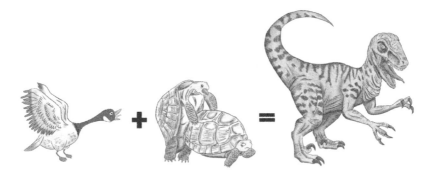

72. The barks the *Velociraptor* characters in *Jurassic Park* made when talking to each other were created by recording the lusty bellows of a tortoise in the throes of passion. The raptors' rasps and hisses were the sounds of angry geese.

73. Over the production run of 1961's *101 Dalmatians* animated feature, the staff had to shade in and animate nearly 6.5 million spots.

74. The 1996 live-action required 20 adult Dalmatians to play Pongo and Perdita (the parents) and 230 Dalmatian puppies. The puppies had to be replaced every 2 weeks because they grew up so fast.

75. The dogs were terrified of Glenn Close when she was in full costume and channeling her inner Cruella DeVil. The dalmatian portraying Perdita was visibly shaking and had to be lured into the set with doggy treats every time.

76. The first game Mario ever featured in was not a *Mario Bros.* game but the 1981 arcade game *Donkey Kong*. In the sequel, *Donkey Kong Jr.*, Mario is the villain.

77. Mario's first love wasn't Peach but Pauline, the damsel in distress in *Donkey Kong*, formerly known as "Lady." Pauline moved on and became the red dressed singer and mayor of New Donk City in *Super Mario Odyssey*.

78. Mario's original name was "Jumpman," and Shigeru Miyamoto (one of the creators) almost renamed him "Mr. Video." "Super Jumpman" and "Mr. Video Kart" aren't exactly catchy.

79. Super Mario was born with a super mustache because Miyamoto wanted to make the 8-bit character more recognizable. Mario also got his signature red hat because it was way too hard to animate hair with the hardware at the time.

80. Mario's name came from the businessman Mario Segale, the landlord of Nintendo of America's office. He didn't sport a thick, luscious 'stache like his pixelated counterpart, but he knew how to get lots of coins.

81. *Super Mario Bros. is dark.* Bowser and his Koopas are turtles that wield black magic to transform the citizens of the Mushroom Kingdom into bricks. This means every time you smash a brick as Mario, you're committing genocide of the Mushroom People... You monster.

82. Boos, the shy ghosts that freeze when you look at them but come at you when you turn your back, were conceived by Takashi Tezuka, the co-creator of Super Mario. He found inspiration after his usually reserved wife had such a big out-burst that it terrified him. He was spending too much time at work, and she was fed up.

83. Yoshi's full name is "T. Yoshisaur Munchakoopas." The "T" is a mystery.

84. The boss character names in the original Japanese version of *Street Fighter II* were swapped for the North American release. The claw-wielding matador we call "Vega" is the actual Balrog. M. Bison, the psychic dictator in red, is the true Vega. And the boxer we know as "Balrog" is the real M. Bison. Only Sagat kept his name.

85. The "M." in M. Bison stands for "Mike." Mike Bison is a tribute to the heavyweight boxing champion, Mike Tyson, but it was changed to "Balrog" in the US version. It might've been to avoid a lawsuit or paying royalties to Tyson, given Bison's likeness to him, or because during the game's release, Tyson was facing sexual assault allegations, so Capcom USA wanted to distance their brand from him.

86. Sagat was inspired by the Muay Thai kickboxing legend Sagat Petchyindee. Of the 317 fights in his professional career, he won more than 150 bouts via knockout. He was known and feared for his devastating leg kicks and face-splitting elbows. He couldn't fire tiger shots, but he had a mean uppercut.

87. Chun-Li is the first-ever playable female character in the history of fighting games. She spinning bird kicked her way into our screens —and into my heart— in 1991 in *Street Fighter II*.

88. Well, actually... Sheng Long was a hoax character. One of Ryu's victory quotes in *Street Fighter II* was, "You must defeat Sheng Long to stand a chance." "Sheng Long" was a mistake by a Chinese translator. It was supposed to be "shoryuken," which means "rising dragon fist" in Japanese. It was corrected in later games.

89. Darth Vader's suit, helmet, and neck guard were inspired by samurai armor. It would cost $18.3 million to build a true-to-life Darth Vader suit that functioned like it would in the movies.

90. The word "Jedi" was borrowed from "Jidaigeki," the Japanese term for samurai period dramas. George Lucas is a huge fan of Akira Kurosawa's *The Hidden Fortress* and took much inspiration from it for *Star Wars*.

91. Well, actually... Darth Vader never said, "Luke, I am your father." The correct quote is, "No, I am your father." Also, "Darth" is the title bestowed upon Sith Lords, and "Vader" means "father" in Dutch.

92. Darth Vader is voiced by James Earl Jones, who played Mufasa in *The Lion King* and King Jaffe in *Coming to America*. Vader's breathing sound effect was made by putting a microphone inside a scuba tank's air regulator.

93. Chewbacca was inspired by George Lucas' late dog, Indiana, an Alaskan malamute, a sled dog. Chewie's signature growl is a combination of bear, badger, lion, and walrus noises.

94. Chewbacca's actor was 7 feet 2 inches (2.2 meters) tall. Peter Mayhew got the role by standing up for his audition.

95. George Lucas almost named Yoda "Buffy." Luckily, it was changed to "Minch Yoda" and eventually shortened to "Yoda." Slay vampires, I must.

96. Both the original Yoda and Miss Piggy were voiced by the same guy, Frank Oz, who also puppeteered them.

97. The "asteroids" of the Millenium Falcon escape scene were spray-painted potatoes. The exogorth, the giant space slug that almost ate the Millenium Falcon, was a hand puppet.

98. Jabba the Hutt was inspired by Sydney Greenstreet, the portly 350-pound (160-kilogram) man who played Signor Ferrari in *Casablanca*. It took 7 puppeteers to bring the gigantic Jabba to life.

99. It took 3 hours to film the *Star Wars* opening text crawl. Computer technology was limited in 1977, so it was impossible to superimpose moving text on a screen. The team had to manually place die-cut yellow letters on top of a big black rectangle and slowly pan the camera downward. Worse yet, it had to be done in multiple languages.

100. The garbage in the compactor scene in *A New Hope* was actual garbage. The smell was so horrible that Mark Hamill (Luke Skywalker) literally burst a blood vessel from holding his breath so much.

101. Though it brought him much fame and fortune, Alec Guinness absolutely despised being Obi-Wan Kenobi. He was so tired of the character that he demanded George Lucas kill his character off.

102. To tap into his inner Jack Sparrow, Johnny Depp took inspiration from 18th-century pirates, who were the rock stars of yesteryear, and modeled his mannerisms after an actual rock star, Keith Richards of The Rolling Stones. Richard played Captain Teague, Sparrow's father.

103. Gore Verbinski, the director of the first three *Pirates of the Caribbean* movies, went to the ends of the world to find the perfect locations. One set in *Dead Man's Chest* was the remote Caribbean island of Dominica, and Verbinski somehow convinced Disney to pave the island so there would be roads to transport equipment. There weren't enough hotel rooms for the 500-person crew, so they had to be flown in daily.

104. There's a deleted scene in the *Curse of the Black Pearl* DVD where Jack Sparrow gets cornered by Barbossa's henchmen and rambles about how the French invented the word "parlay" and created mayonnaise. In response to this revelation, the bald and portly Pintel (Lee Arenberg) replies, "I like mayonnaise." Because of this single innocent line, Arenberg has been cursed to occasionally receive a jar of mayonnaise from die-hard fans whenever he's seen in public.

105. The chiseled abs of the *300* actors were 100% real. No CGI was used. The 8-week diet and weight training were as demanding as an actual Spartan's training program. Probably. Gerard Butler said it was the hardest thing he ever did.

106. The 2007 movie *300* was adapted from the 1998 graphic novel by Frank Miller of the same name, which was inspired by Rudolph Maté's *The 300 Spartans* (1962), which was based on the Battle of Thermopylae as told by Herodotus, the Greek father of history, around 480 BCE.

107. In the original Frank Miller comic, the iconic line "This is Sparta!" was not yelled out; it was spoken calmly but firmly. The "This is SPAR-TA!" techno remix meme was made in 2007... Don't you feel old?

108. The word "meme" was invented in 1976 by Richard Dawkins before the internet was even accessible. A meme is a means of spreading culture, ideas, and information. Music, fairy tales, and cave drawings are memes.

109. The "Cool S," the "Suzuki S," the "Superman S," the "Stussy S." This mysterious symbol millennial school kids would scribble all over their notebooks and bathroom stalls goes by many names, but no one really knows where it came from. It just caught on because it was fun to draw.

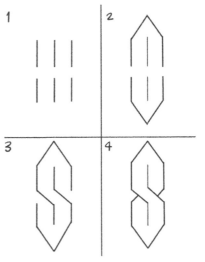

110. The "Cool S" is an example of a Moebius strip, a looped shape resembling a strip of paper attached at the ends and given a half-twist. M.C. Escher, famous for *Relativity*, that art with the mind-melting stairs, also used Moebius strips in his works.

111. Memento mori, "Remember that you must die," is also a meme, and so is Carpe diem, "Seize the day."

112. The first viral internet meme was *Baby Cha-Cha-Cha*, an uncanny valley 3D dancing baby conceived by Kinetix Character Studio in 1996.

113. "Mr. T Ate My Balls" is the first macro, a meme with a still image and text. Nehal Patel, a student from the University of Illinois, had the revolutionary idea of replacing the speech bubble on a Mr. T comic book panel in 1997.

114. The first emoji, the yellow and black smiley face, was created in 1963 by the graphic designer Harvey Ball... Where would we be without him?

115. The true identity of Scumbag Steve, the last guy you would want to bring 10 of his weird friends to your house party uninvited, is Blake Boston. His image was first used on the album cover of his hip-hop group, Beantown Mafia... No joke, the meme kinda ruined this guy's life.

116. Success Kid, the little boy clenching his fist with a victorious grin, did indeed become successful. Sammy Griner leveraged his internet fame to raise funds for his father's kidney transplant.

117. Before it was a gag on *Family Guy*, featured in *The Proud Family*, and became the dance track for an overly enthusiastic banana, *Peanut Butter Jelly Time* was an actual song by The Buckwheat Boyz.

118. Philosoraptor, an extinct creature that ponders the big questions about life, was a T-shirt design before becoming an internet sensation. This clever girl was created by Sam Smith (not the famous singer).

119. Well, actually... Dramatic Chipmunk isn't a chipmunk or a gopher; it's a prairie dog. The clip of the suspicious rodent originated in Japan in the 2000s during a segment featuring cute animals on *Hello! Morning*, a weekly show.

120. The Doge meme came into existence after a Japanese kindergarten teacher uploaded a perfectly timed picture of her Shiba Inu side-eyeing the camera. Doge is a female, and her name is Kabosu. A kabosu is a green-skinned Japanese citrus fruit related to yuzu and bitter orange.

Chapter 8

Far Out Space and Science Facts

Science is constantly changing. What's considered true today gets proven false tomorrow, and a new truth arises. Your development as a person works the same way.

Just when you think you know how the world works, something happens that makes you reevaluate what you fundamentally believe to be true. Compare your understanding of the world from when you were a teen versus when you were in college versus now that you're a working adult with responsibilities.

Over time, you discovered new things and recalibrated your perception of truth. The only certainty is that you'll shift your paradigm again. Like your scope of reality, the universe is getting bigger, and technology is getting better. In this chapter, you'll learn that there are more than three states of matter, that diamonds aren't the hardest substance, and that the sun isn't the hottest thing ever.

You'll also discover peculiar things like the insane lengths astronauts go through to use the toilet, the weird reason our galaxy is called the "Milky Way," and the origins of mind-boggling technologies you mindlessly use every day.

***

1. If you dip your hand in a jug of water, the water level will rise, but if you drop in a handful of salt, the water level will go down. This happens because the salt rearranges the water molecules into a more organized and compact configuration.

2. Well, actually... There are more than 3 states of matter. Lightning, for example, is a plasma, the fourth state. Some scientists suggest there might be as many as 22 other states.

3. The drinking glass you pour your liquids into is also a liquid... Sort of. Glass is an amorphous solid; its molecules flow like a liquid but move so slow that you can't notice it flowing. Old glass windows look like they're melting because of shoddy glass making.

4. Under very specific conditions in a vacuum, water can be solid, liquid, and gas simultaneously. This is known as the "Triple Point" effect... If water, vapor, and ice can peacefully coexist without trying to change each other, so can we.

5. Lightning can create ozone, the gas that protects us Earthlings from the Sun's ultraviolet rays. Lightning literally splits oxygen molecules (O_2) in half into single atoms. To stabilize themselves, they frantically recombine into ozone (O_3).

6. That crisp, clean scent you get after a thunderstorm or when you're near a crashing waterfall is caused by ozone, which smells similar to chlorine.

7. Though you can't see it floating in the air, oxygen is light blue. It's visible only when cooled to a liquid or a solid.

8. Well, actually... Trees don't make the most oxygen. More than half of our breathable O_2 comes from the ocean. You can thank the plankton and seaweed underwater for us not suffocating on land.

9. There are more trees on Earth than stars in the Milky Way. Our galaxy has a measly 100-400 billion stars, while our planet has 3 trillion trees.

10. 10-15% of The Milky Way is just dust, gas, and some toxic space grease. Grease contains carbon, which may indicate life on faraway planets. We've only discovered 0.000003% of our galaxy, so who knows what, or who, is out there.

11. The universe is big (gasp). The Milky Way alone is so ridiculously huge that it would take light, which travels at a speed of 186,000 miles per second (300,000 kilometers per second), 2 million years to travel across it. Our galaxy is much, much larger than the previously thought 100,000-200,000 lightyears, and it's still growing.

12. The Milky Way is almost as old as the universe. The most recent estimate of the Universe's age is 13.7 billion years, and the Milky way is just 0.1 billion years shy.

13. The Milky Way galaxy got its name from Hera, Zeus' wife, after she squirted breast milk across the sky. Yup. The Greek myth goes that Zeus snuck baby Heracles (Hercules) into Hera's room and had him suckle on her while she was asleep. The goddess woke up and, in shock, pushed the little bastard away (because Heracles was Zeus' illegitimate son), and, well, some accidental spillage occurred.

14. Over 20 million asteroids fall on Earth every day. It would take just a single mile-wide (1.6 kilometer-wide) asteroid to cause a mass extinction, but luckily, the vast majority fizzle out as they fall. If an Earth-shattering rock were to reach us, though, all the nukes in the world wouldn't be enough to stop it. It's been about 66 million years since the last extinction, though, so we are overdue.

15. Like Earth, the storms on most other planets in our solar system look round or oval from above. On the north pole Saturn, though, there's a storm raging that looks like a hexagon from above. Scientists call this storm "The Hexagon." They suspect this warped shape is caused by Saturn's smaller storms violently colliding with the larger storms within.

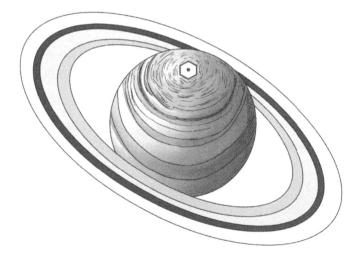

16. Well, actually... Saturn isn't blue. The only blue part of Saturn is its north pole. For the most part, the ringed planet is pale yellow with bands of tan, brown, and orange.

17. The International Astronomical Union names all the mountains on Titan, Saturn's biggest moon, after the fictional mountains of *The Lord of the Rings*. There's the Doom Mons, the Erebor Mons, and the Misty Montes, to name a few.

18. Saturn has 7 rings that stretch out 75,000 miles (121,000 kilometers) away from the planet and are only 65 feet (20 meters) thick. Unfortunately, you can't walk on them because they're made of floating ice, rocks, and dust.

19. Jupiter has rings, but they're hard to see because they're not made of ice, which reflects light. They're made of space dust, which doesn't shine.

20. The largest moon in the solar system belongs to Jupiter. The moon Ganymede has a diameter of 3,275 miles (5,270 kilometers), surpassing Mercury in size.

21. Uranus is a gas giant, and so are Saturn, Jupiter, and Neptune. Despite their astronomical size, their mostly gas compositions make them less dense than water. If you had a large enough swimming pool, you could swim right beside Saturn. At least for a while before it evaporated into the air.

22. Jupiter was named after the Roman king of the gods (aka Zeus in Greek myth). This gargantuan gas giant is so huge that it could fit all the other planets in our solar system twice over. In Earth terms, Jupiter could accommodate 11 Earths.

23. "You'll never be a star!" This is what my father told me as a child and what astronomers told Jupiter. Despite its enormous size and abundance of helium and hydrogen, it's said that Jupiter doesn't have what it takes to reach stardom. It would have to multiply its mass by 80 times to exert enough gravity needed to achieve nuclear fusion... Hang in there, Jupiter, we'll prove them wrong one day.

24. Jupiter's "Great Red Spot" alone is twice as big as Earth. The GRS is a giant storm that has been raging for at least 350 years. It's been steadily shrinking, so it won't be long before it's the diameter of Earth, 8,000 miles (13,000 kilometers).

25. One year on Jupiter is about 12 years on Earth, which is how long it takes for the king of planets to orbit the Sun. Confoundingly, Jupiter spins so fast on its axis that one day lasts less than 10 hours. Because of its slight 3° tilt, Jupiter doesn't experience seasons. Our 4-seasoned Earth is angled 23°.

26. Lasers were used to measure the distance between the Earth and the Moon. During the Apollo 11 Mission, astronauts placed reflectors on the Moon's surface, and NASA fired lasers all the way from Earth and hit their exact location... Talk about precision engineering!

27. The space between the Earth and the Moon is about 240,000 miles (390,000 kilometers). You could squeeze all the planets in our solar system, Jupiter included, in between them and still have space left over to squeeze in an extra half a Mercury.

28. If you were to drive straight to the Moon at 70 miles per hour (110 kilometers per hour) without taking any bathroom breaks, it would take you 9 years to reach it.

29. Instead of water, it rains solid diamonds on Jupiter and Saturn. This happens because the atmospheric pressure of these planets is so intense that it crushes airborne carbon atoms into diamonds. It rains 2.2 million pounds (1 million kilograms) of diamonds, or more, every year.

30. There's a white dwarf in space called "Lucy," and it's the largest known diamond in existence. Lucy is about the size of Earth, and her core is a pure diamond weighing 10 billion trillion trillion carats —that's not a typo. They named this diamond in the sky "Lucy" as a clever reference to the Beatles' *Lucy in the Sky with Diamonds*.

31. Diamonds are forever. The youngest natural diamond on Earth is hundreds of millions of years old, and the oldest is at least 3.5 billion years of age.

32. The oldest known planet is "The Genesis Planet." It's been floating around for 12.7 billion years. Planet Earth is just 4.5 billion years old.

33. You are more than 13 billion years old. Well, the hydrogen that makes up your corporeal existence is. Hydrogen was the first chemical element created after the Big Bang, which means everything is hydrogen, in one way or another.

34. Well, actually... Diamond isn't the hardest substance in the world; it's graphene, a synthetic carbon compound. Diamonds aren't even the hardest natural mineral; wurtzite boron nitride and lonsdaleite are stronger. Also, diamond isn't unbreakable; smashing it with a regular hammer will shatter it into tiny pieces... Araki lied.

35. Every time you light a candle, you produce 1.5 million nanoscopic diamonds. If you don't have a candle handy, peanut butter can do in a pinch. All you need is a crushing machine that can simulate the extreme heat and pressure of the earth's mantle and squish the carbon-rich peanut butter into diamonds.

36. For just a couple thousand dollars, you can turn your loved ones into wearable jewelry. This process involves incinerating your dead cat and/or grandmother and then compressing their carbon-rich ashes into a cremation diamond... I guess you could call them "dead ringers."

37. The Sun's core is insanely powerful. If you could extract just a pinhead-sized piece of the Sun's core, it would be strong enough to burn up everything and everyone within a 90-mile (145-kilometer) radius.

38. If the Sun were to suddenly disappear in the daytime, it would take 8 minutes and 17 seconds for the world to go dark. That's precisely how long it takes for a ray of sunlight to reach Earth.

39. Well, actually... The Sun is white, just like the Moon in space. It only looks yellow, orange, or red throughout the day because our atmosphere diffuses incoming light. If you want to get technical, the Sun is every color because white is all colors combined, all light wavelengths, visible to the human eye.

40. If you ever wondered why the Sun, even though it's 400 times larger, looks like it's the same size as the Moon, it's because your eyes are playing tricks on you. The Sun is 400 times farther from Earth than the Moon is, so it skews your perception of size and scale.

41. The very same cameras used during the first landing on the Moon in 1969 are still up there. To clear room for Moon rocks, astronauts in the Apollo 11 mission had to leave 12 Hasselblad cameras behind.

42. The first digital camera weighed 8 pounds (3.6 kilograms) and had a resolution of 0.01 megapixels. It was built in 1975 by Steven Sasson while working for Kodak... By the way, "Kodak" doesn't mean anything. George Eastman, the founder, thought the letter "K" was kinda kool.

43. According to science, your left side is your good side in pictures. The left side of your face is better at displaying emotion, making you look more appealing.

44. Before cameras had convenient little lights embedded in them, flash photography was quite dangerous. Potassium chloride and aluminum powder had to be ignited to create a bright explosion, potentially leading to severe facial burns, permanent hearing damage, or the loss of fingers if the user got careless.

45. Solar flares are absurdly destructive. These explosions release 100 megatons of energy, the equivalent of 2 Soviet-era Tsar Bombas, the most dangerous bomb detonated so far, or about 5,000 Fat Mans. Remember that just 1 Fat Man was enough to decimate Nagasaki.

46. The Sun travels about 450,000 miles per hour (72,000 kilometers per hour). Despite that, it would take this speedy star 225 million years to do a full lap around the Milky Way.

47. Not every planet orbits the Sun. There are several billion "rogue planets," unbound by gravity, aimlessly floating about in space.

48. The Universe is 5% matter, 25% dark matter, and 70% dark energy. They're "dark" because they don't emit their own light or interact with light from other sources, so we can't see them.

49. Well, actually... Space isn't a perfect vacuum devoid of matter. Every cubic meter is occupied by a whole three or so atoms. On Earth, each cubic meter contains about 2.5 x 1025. That's the number 25 followed by 25 zeroes!

50. Due to low gravity in space, astronauts lose a lot of muscle. Their hearts also shrink because they don't have to work as hard to pump blood. On the bright side, there's much less pressure on their spines so they get taller. A similar thing happens to you here on Earth. Your spine decompresses as you sleep, so you're always a bit taller in the morning.

51. No one can hear you burp in space. You literally can't. On Earth, where there's gravity, liquids and solids in your stomach are weighed down and separated from your gasses. If you try to burp in space, you will barf.

52. Astronauts need to be potty trained. The last thing you'd want is to be trapped in a spaceship with feces floating around. Trainees have to practice pooping into a 4-inch (10-centimeter) wide toilet equipped with a camera inside that records the whole process for careful review. Astronauts need to strap themselves to the receptacle to learn how to position themselves, so nothing flies away.

53. Urinating inside a spaceship is a whole other thing. Males and females must place a small cone on their genitals, then hook it up to a hose and vacuum system to suction the liquid into a tank. The men have to be extra careful.

54. If astronauts feel the urge to pee during a spacewalk, they can shamelessly relieve themselves in their spacesuits. Their suits come equipped with special compartments, so the contents won't slosh around in their helmets.

55. Astronauts wear two main suits during missions. The orange "launch and entry suit" is used inside the spaceship whenever they fly or make a landing, and the white "Extravehicular Mobility Unit" is used to exit the spacecraft when in space. EMUs are specifically white because white reflects heat and prevents overheating.

56. You can survive 15 seconds in space without a spacesuit on. At the 16th second, your lungs will inflate like a balloon, and you will die of asphyxiation.

57. EMU spacesuits plus their life-support backpacks weigh 280 pounds (130 kilograms). They're weightless in space, but that doesn't make it easier. It takes 45 minutes to put on an EMU, and after that, users must wait an additional hour inside for oxygen to fill the suit and adjust themselves to the lower pressure.

58. EMU spacesuits are incredibly tough. They can resist direct exposure to the Sun's radiation, adapt to extreme temperatures of -250°F to 250°F (-160°C to 120°C), and can withstand getting hit by sharp debris flying at them at 17,000 miles per hour (27,000 kilometers per hour).

59. The hottest temperature in the universe can be found right here on Earth, and it's achieved by the Large Hadron Collider, a machine that accelerates particles to near lightspeed and crashes them against each other. The point of it is to help physicists better understand the nature of matter and the universe itself. Due to its insane power output, the LHC heats up to a ridiculous 5.5 trillion K, or 9.9 trillion °F (5.5 trillion °C), which is 350,000 times hotter than the Sun.

60. The average temperature of the universe is 2.7 Kelvin, or about -455°F (-270°C). It's speculated that at the peak of the Big Bang, the universe was at a scorching 10 septillion K. That's 25 zeroes, folks.

61. Absolute zero is the coldest temperature imaginable. At zero K, or -459.67°F (-273.15°C), atoms would freeze in place. Achieving this theoretical temperature would require an infinite amount of energy and a perfectly still environment. An atom could only reach absolute zero if it were to be removed from the universe or for the universe itself to disappear and leave the atom in perfect isolation.

62. The coldest temperature in the current universe can be found right here on Earth. Researchers at the Massachusetts Institute of Technology (MIT) almost reached absolute zero (off by less than a billionth of a degree) by cooling sodium gas with a laser beam.

63. The Large Hadron Collider is also the biggest machine in the world, measuring an extensive 17 miles (27 kilometers). Its not-so-top-secret location is at CERN, the European Organization for Nuclear Research, near Geneva, Switzerland.

64. The world's largest nuclear bunker is located in Lucerne, Switzerland, in the Sonnenberg Tunnel. It spans 5,100 feet (1,550 meters) and has enough room to house 20,000 people. There are also enough shelters spread throughout the country to accommodate its entire population, should the need arise. Even farms in Switzerland have them.

65. The World Wide Web was invented at CERN by computer scientist and knight Tim Berners-Lee in 1989. Sir Lee also created HTML and made the first webpage. The URL is http://info.cern.ch, and it still works.

66. The first and now oldest .com domain was registered in 1985. S ymbolics.com, the website of the now-defunct Symbolics computer corporation, remains operational.

67. The internet was invented in 1969 by the Advanced Research Projects Agency Network (ARPANET) to link military computers together and facilitate information sharing. The internet only became available to civilians in 1991.

68. Email existed before the Web. The first email ever was sent in 1974 by Computer Scientist Ray Tomlinson, who emailed himself. He doesn't remember what he wrote.

69. The first spam email was an ad to sell computers. It was sent by Gary Thuerk in 1978. Spam now accounts for 70-80% of all emails sent... Thanks, Gary. Not!

70. Virtually all the internet data in the world is transmitted through a vast network of undersea cables. Internet data weighs 2 ounces (60 grams), as much as an egg.

71. There's a contingency plan for if a worldwide disaster were to ever shut down the internet, seven secret members of the Internet Corporation for Assigned Names and Numbers (ICANN) who hold the seven keys will join forces and meet in an undisclosed location to reboot the internet.

72. The term "wifi" has no inherent meaning. "Wi" is an abbreviation of "wireless," but "fi" doesn't mean "fidelity," or anything. The inventor, Phil Belanger, just called it "Wi-Fi" because it sounded cool like "Hi-Fi" (High Fidelity) for music.

73. Wifi will be eventually phased out and replaced by LiFi. LiFi uses light, making it 100 times faster than wifi, which uses radio waves.

74. Bluetooth is also a radio-based technology. The Bluetooth logo is a combination of the Danish Viking runes for "H" and "B," which came from the Danish King Harald "Bluetooth" Gormsson, whose tooth got blue from decay.

75. Microwave ovens work by vibrating the water molecules in your food to create heat. The food is cooked from the surface, and the heat slowly spreads inwards. Microwaves can only penetrate about an inch (2.54 centimeters) deep, which is why it's generally safe to microwave raw bacon strips but not a whole chicken.

76. Well, actually... Microwaves won't destroy all the nutrients in your food. No more than any other cooking method will, at least. In some cases, microwaving may even preserve food nutrition because of the faster cooking time. Boiling vegetables, for example, causes their vitamins to leak out into the water.

77. It's a bad idea to microwave metal, like a stainless steel fork, because it attracts and reflects microwaves, making sparks fly and burning your microwave. Metal is such an excellent electrical conductor because its electrons are constantly shifting.

78. Lasers are strong enough to slice through plastic, wood, and metal. They could easily cut a human in half à la James Bond, but can also be used for less nefarious deeds like removing cancerous tumors and to perform brain surgery.

79. Lasers have an extreme precision of less than 1 nanometer. Laser-based optical tweezers are so pinpoint-accurate that they can pull DNA strands apart and separate them into their individual components.

80. Human beings do, in fact, have auras. You emit your own natural light, but it's too weak to see without specialized equipment. There's nothing mystical or celestial about auras. Squids and fireflies have them, too, but it's called "bioluminescence." Sorry hippies, your star children, indigo children, or whatever you call them, don't have any special powers. They're as mundane and average as the rest of us.

Chapter 9

All-Star Sports Facts

I'll be honest. I don't really care about sports. There. I said it.

But don't worry, sports fans, I won't leave you hanging. Get your game on because you're going to learn some spectacular sports trivia and discover the most bizarre athlete superstitions and good luck rituals. If you're like me, though, and don't pay much attention to football, baseball, or even the Olympics, read this chapter anyway.

Have you ever been at a loss for words when people started talking to you about sports? Well, keep reading because there are some very useful words here.

Pretty much anything can be a sport. If it involves two or more competitors, it's a sport. And let me tell you, people play real fast and loose with this term.

***

1. The Aztecs combined their love of blood and sport to make Ulla-maliztli, aka "the Mesoamerican ballgame." Players would bounce a large, heavy rubber ball with their elbows, hips, knees, and heads and send it through upright stone hoops attached to walls to score points. Historians aren't sure if it was the losers or the winners who would be sacrificed after the game. The skulls of past players decorated the arena.

2. Aztec city-states sometimes used the ballgame to settle their differences and avoid civil wars. Blood would still be spilled, but at least they wouldn't lose all their valuable soldiers.

3. Even without the risk of becoming an offering to Quetzalcóatl, the ballgame was still dangerous. Non-sacrificial players often left the game riddled with bruises and broken bones, and death on the court was not uncommon. A modern, toned-down version of the sport, Ulama, is practiced in Mexico. A variation of Ulama is featured in the animated movie The Road to El Dorado.

4. Until 1939, it was optional for American football players to wear helmets. Instead of headgear, old-school players would grow their hair out, believing their soft, fluffy locks would be enough to protect them against head trauma.

5. Well, actually... Despite the nickname, footballs were never made of pigskin. The first footballs were inflated pigs' bladders stuffed with straw or cloth. Modern footballs are made of vulcanized rubber, air, and cow leather.

6. Only 1 out of every 1.09 million high schoolers make it as professional football players. In comparison, 1 out of every 17.4 million cows ever make it as professional footballs. Talk about stiff competition.

7. The official nickname of the NFL football is "The Duke." It was named after Wellington Timothy Mara, who was in turn named after the Duke of Wellington.

8. The technical term for a football's shape is a "prolate spheroid." The first footballs were round and resembled walnuts, then had a shape similar to rugby balls, then took on a sleeker, more aerodynamic form.

9. The practice of huddling in football started because of a partly deaf university player named Paul Hubbard, who needed to hear the game plan without it being overheard by the other team.

10. The average NFL broadcast lasts 3 hours, but the ball is only in play for 18 of those 180 minutes. The remaining 90% of the time is spent on replays, huddles, stoppages, commercials, and shots of players walking from one spot to another.

11. Fans of the Green Bay Packers are ravenous. Season tickets have been completely sold out every season and will be for the next 1,000 years. Many Packers fans refuse to part with their golden tickets even if offered large sums of money... I hope you guys get like that with my books after I die and that my works become your priceless treasures, lovingly framed on a wall right beside your family photos.

12. The average NFL player's career lasts only 3.3 years. Running backs have the shortest run of 2.6 years, and punters go the longest at 4.9 years. Whatever the position, 80% of ex-NFL players go bankrupt within just 2 years of retiring.

13. The youngest NFL Hall of Famer is Gale Sayers, who was inducted at age 34. The oldest is Ed Sabol, who was enshrined at 94 —60 years apart.

14. In his obituary, one frustrated football fan requested that he be carried in his coffin by six players of the Cleveland Browns, so his team could let him down one last time.

15. Championship shirts are made ahead of time for both teams facing off at the Superbowl finals. Naturally, the losing team can't sell their premade victory jerseys in America, so the unsold garments are donated to the Dominican Republic instead.

16. It's not just the champions that get Superbowl rings. Referees and the runners-up also receive their own custom-made Superbowl rings. Of course, no self-respecting player would want to wear their ring of defeat in public, though.

17. Chuck Howley, the linebacker of the Cowboys, is the first and only player to be awarded the Super Bowl MVP prize while playing for the losing team.

18. The Miami Dolphins are the only team to play a perfect season with zero losses in Super Bowl history. The living members of the 1972 Dolphins have a long-standing tradition of meeting up to drink champagne whenever the team with the longest win streak in the current season loses its first game.

19. Deion Sanders is the only athlete in sports history to score a touchdown in the NFL and bat a home run in the MLB in the same week.

20. Gaylord Perry's manager declared that they (NASA) would land a man on the Moon before Perry hit a home run. Lo and behold, Perry hit a home run less than an hour after Neil Armstrong landed on the Moon.

21. The Angels, the Dodgers, and the Yankees are the few MLB teams that don't have an official mascot. The Yankees did once, but fans got so angry that they physically assaulted the guy in the suit... Rest in peace, Dandy. We barely knew you.

22. By MLB regulation, all Umpires must wear black underwear, just in case their pants rip mid-game... After all, it would be very embarrassing to have your questionably stained tighty whities broadcast to millions of viewers.

23. Umpires and clubhouse attendants in the MLB have to rub 72 brand-new baseballs in mud before every game. New baseballs are slippery and difficult to throw, so they need to be roughed up in advance. This particular mud can only be found in New Jersey, and its exact location is a heavily guarded secret.

24. During the Battle of the Bulge in WWII, American soldiers would quiz each other's baseball knowledge to sniff out German spies masquerading as American G.I.s.

25. Until 1934, pitchers were allowed to drench their balls (baseballs) in as much spit as possible to make them slick and hard to hit. It was technically banned in 1920, but a handful of veteran pitchers were permitted to do it until they retired.

26. Retired MLB players Jorge Posada and Moises Alou were notorious for urinating on their hands during practice. They believed it made their skin rougher and thus improved their grip on the ball... They banned spitballs, but not this?

27. While preparing for his 1999 season with the Houston Astros, Moises Alou fell off a treadmill and tore his ACL, putting his knee out of commission that year. The following year, he hurt his knee again after tripping over his son and was forced to miss the season's first weeks.

28. Charlie Sheen once bought 2,615 tickets to a game at Anaheim Stadium just so he could run around and catch a home run ball. No one hit a homerun for ol' Charlie that day.

29. Richard "Richie" Ashburn once hit a foul ball that struck a woman in the crowd and broke her nose. He batted another foul soon after and hit her again while being carried out on a stretcher.

30. Even during Michael Jordan's short and unsuccessful stint as a baseball player, Jerry Reinsdorf, the owner of the Chicago Bulls, still paid him his NBA salary of $4 million... It's almost like he knew Michael Jordan would fail and come running back.

31. Babe Ruth stuffed cabbage leaves under his hat to keep cool during baseball games. He would swap in a new one, of which he kept in an ice box, every other inning.

32. 32 is a lucky number. Yankees catcher Elston Howard, Dodgers pitcher Sandy Koufax in the MLB, and Cleveland Browns' running back Jim Brown in the NFL all got the Most Valuable Player award in 1963 wearing the number 32.

33. Pitcher John "Turk" Wendell was a superstitious fellow. He would brush his teeth and munch on licorice every inning for good luck... Just drinking OJ after brushing your teeth is nasty. Imagine it with licorice.

34. There's a Japanese urban legend that the Hanshin Tigers baseball team has been cursed by the vengeful ghost of Colonel Sanders. After winning in 1985, fans rioted and threw Sander's KFC storefront statue into a river. After that, the Hanshin Tigers had a two-decades-long losing streak, supposedly thanks to the Curse of the Colonel.

35. Well, actually... The MLB never scouted Fidel Castro, and his fastball wasn't nearly fast enough for the big leagues. Ironically, the communist dictator loved capitalist America's favorite pastime. Baseball is the national sport of Cuba.

36. Despite its association with the wealthy, golf started out as a simple pastime for Scottish shepherds around the 14th-15th centuries. It involved hitting a rock or a piece of dried sheep dung with a crook (a stick with a hook at the end) towards a target, sometimes a wall, or a cup or mug placed on the ground. Golf eventually gained its prestigious reputation thanks to King James IV of Scotland, who liked playing it in his spare time.

37. Polo, another sport typically reserved for the wealthy, has been taken down a peg in Germany. Instead of a horse and mallet, teams of 3-5 riders smack a ball around with hockey sticks while awkwardly pedaling themselves on unicycles.

38. King James IV's pre-predecessor, King James II, outlawed golf during his rule. There was a war to be fought in 1457 Scotland, but the soldiers skipped out on training to play golf, so James II banned the distraction. The Scots didn't care and snuck in some tee time when he wasn't looking.

39. Mary Queen of the Scots was also a fan of golf and probably the first woman to play it. During her time in France in the 15th century, she brought her own golf gear to play with the other royalty. On a side note, the term "caddy" came from the French cadets who would guard them and carry their clubs throughout the course.

40. The average golf ball has 336 dimples. These tiny craters make the ball more aerodynamic, letting it fly farther and faster, and improving the shot's accuracy.

41. Upon impact, golf balls can reach speeds over 170 miles per hour (275 kilometers per hour).

42. The average golfer has a 1 in 12,500 chance of sinking a hole-in-one. Many pro golfers go their entire careers without making a hole-in-one, but Tiger Woods scored his first of many at just 8 years old.

43. Golf holes never stay in one place for long. The cups (golf holes) are constantly shifted throughout the day to keep the greens (grass) healthy and to ensure the cups stay at a consistent size and shape.

44. Golf, along with the javelin throw, are the first sports ever played on the Moon. Astronaut Alan Shepard Jr. went out of his way to bring golf balls, clubs, and tees into space just to say he did it. According to him, one of them went into a Moon crater, and the other "sailed for miles and miles."

45. Well, actually... The official distance of a marathon is 26.2 miles (42.2 kilometers), and it was established in the 1908 London Olympics. It has no connection to the story of a Greek messenger who ran from the village of Marathon to Athens and died of exhaustion. The distance between those locations is less than 25 miles (40 kilometers).

46. No one, to date, has ever died of dehydration while running a marathon. Many runners have kicked the bucket by drinking too much water for fear of getting dehydrated.

47. Listening to music while running has been proven to make you a better runner. Music gets you in the zone and helps you maintain a consistent pace as your feet hit the ground in sync with your beats.

48. American marathoner Frederick Lorz was the first to finish the marathon of the 1904 summer Olympics in St. Louis. It was later discovered that he cheated. He sneakily hopped into a car mid-race and was driven by his coach, then got off and ran a bit to make it look like he won fair and square.

49. The first black athlete to win a gold medal in the marathon was Abebe Bikila during the Rome summer Olympics of 1960. The Ethiopian legend beat his competition by a large margin... And he did it barefoot! It took Bikila 40 days to recover. He made another appearance in the 1964 Tokyo summer Olympics, but this time with shoes. Bikila was the first person to win the marathon twice.

50. Jesse Owens broke four world records in track-and-field in under 45 minutes. In 1935, Owens conquered the long jump, the 100-yard dash, the 220-yard dash, and the 220-yard low hurdles... Quite the feet, indeed.

51. Speed walking is an Olympic sport. The "athletes" are known as "Race Walkers," and they waddle with stiff legs and wiggle their butts for a whole 30 miles (50 kilometers).

52. Steeplechase, with humans, is also an Olympic event. It's essentially a 1,865-mile (3,000 kilometers) track-and-field race, but with hurdles with puddles of water.

53. Tug-of-war was an Olympic event between 1900 and 1920. And so was architecture from 1912 to 1948.

54. Solo synchronized swimming was once part of the Olympics in 1984, 1988, and 1992. It took the biggest brains in the committee 8 years to realize synchronized swimming looks ridiculous if there isn't anyone to synchronize to... What's next? Solo badminton?

55. Another odd water sport was obstacle swimming in the Paris 1900 Olympics. Olympians had to climb a pole, go over a row of boats, then swim under more boats.

56. Paris 1900 also graced its spectators with competitive poodle clipping. 128 participants had to artistically trim the fur of as many poodles as possible within 2 hours. The victor completed 17 trimmings... What I want to know is how they got so many poodles to sit still.

57. The interlaced Olympic rings are specifically colored black, blue, red, yellow, and green to be inclusive of all nations (that weren't banned). Every country has at least one of the five Olympic colors in its flag.

58. China didn't win any Olympic medals until 1984. Finally, in the 2008 Beijing games, their teams won a combined 100 medals. They sure made their home country proud... I wish I could say the same about Brazil in the 2014 FIFA World Cup. 7-1 (cough, cough). Germany (cough, cough).

59. Usain Bolt exclusively ate McDonald's chicken nuggets during the Beijing Olympics. Being far from home, it was the only familiar food he could trust wouldn't get him sick. Bolt won three gold medals despite his all chicken nuggy diet.

60. After an American won the gold in the pole-vaulting during the 1936 Berlin Olympics, two Japanese athletes, Sueo Oe and Shuhei Nishida, were tied for second place. As a show of respect for each other's efforts, they refused to compete against each other, despite the judges' demands. Upon returning, they had the silver and bronze medals cut in half and then welded into a pair of mixed medals.

61. The Tokyo 2020 Olympic medals were made of recycled material. Scraps of precious metals (bronze, silver, and gold) were extracted from discarded cell phones, cameras, and computer parts and then melted to produce thousands of medals.

62. Olympic gold medals haven't been made of pure gold since 1912. It depends on the country, but generally, first place medals are 92.5% silver with gold plating. Also, bronze medals aren't bronze; they're 95% copper and 5% zinc. Only silver medals are entirely made of silver.

63. Michael Phelps has won more gold medals than 97 countries have individually. 23. If he were to establish his own nation, it would be in 35th place as far as gold medals are concerned.

64. Michael Phelps was terrified of putting his head underwater as a kid. Because of that, young Michael hated swimming. If it weren't for his family pressuring him to swim, he would have never grown up to become a famous and successful Olympian... Peer pressure isn't always bad, is it?

65. Besides being naturally gifted and having an insane work ethic, Phelps also has a disproportionate physical advantage. He has long arms, long feet, a tall torso, and short legs. At 6 feet 2 inches (193 centimeters) long, Phelps has the torso of a man 4 inches (10 centimeters) taller than him and the legs of a man 8 inches (20 centimeters) smaller... His wonky body is literally perfect for high-speed swimming.

66. During training season, Michael Phelps consumed 12,000 calories every day. "What did he eat?" Too many things to list.

67. The oldest sports in history are running and wrestling. They date as far back as 15,300 years ago during the Upper Paleolithic era. The earliest depictions of these sports come from ancient France, not Greece, surprisingly.

68. Pro wrestling is fake, but the injuries are real. Due to all the damage they take and the substances they take to keep training, their careers are often short. 49 out of 62 wrestlers don't make it to age 50.

69. When the script called for blood, wrestlers cut their foreheads with a razor blade they stashed in their wristbands. To the dismay of blood-thirsty fans, the WWE banned the practice of blading, and matches are paused whenever there's accidental bleeding.

70. The biggest live audience for a wrestling event was 150,000 people, and it was held in Pyongyang, North Korea. The show was spearheaded by American promotion WCW and Japanese promotion NJPW in 1995. North Korean citizens were "invited" (forced) by the Supreme Leader to attend the event.

71. Lucha libre (Mexican pro wrestling) tradition dictates that luchadores must always wear their masks, even outside the ring. Removing your opponent's mask during a match is grounds for disqualification. Luchadores occasionally engage in mask-versus-mask bouts in which the loser is forced to take their own mask off and take on a new identity.

72. One of the most legendary luchadores was the silver mask-clad El Santo. He broke tradition by revealing his face once during a talk show and strangely passed away a week later. His last request was to be buried with his mask on.

73. The world's greatest sport, according to some Russians, is competitive face slapping. In this simple and brutal sport, two combatants stand in front of each other and take turns slapping the other until one of them gives up or is knocked out. It doesn't have weight classes.

74. The manliest sport, even more so than Russian face slapping, is lumberjacking. At the Lumberjack World Championships in Wisconsin, contestants climb trees, saw down trees, roll logs, and more. Even the women participating get man cards.

75. Leave it to the British to turn toe wrestling into an actual sport. Frustrated that England wasn't the best in the world at any sport at the time, in 1976, some bloke and his mates invented toe wrestling. Competitors lock their big toes together and attempt to push the other's foot sideways to pin it down, similar to arm wrestling.

76. Matt Stutzman set the record for the farthest bow and arrow shot in the history of the Olympics —all Olympics. He hit his target from 930 feet (283 meters) away. And he did it with his feet, because he was born without arms. What an absolute legend!

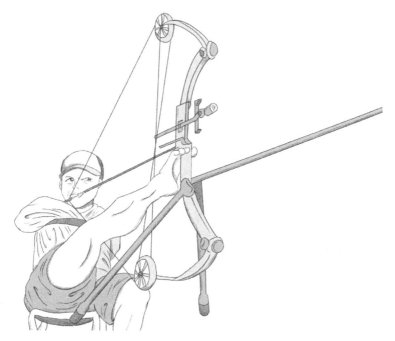

77. Vikings were one of the first people to ski for fun. They even had a specific god of skiing named "Ullr."

78. Spitting watermelon seeds, bobbing for pigs' feet, belly-flopping in the mud, throwing toilet seats for distance, and making sweet, sweet melodies with your armpit farts. You know you're a redneck if any of that sounds appealing to you. Well, at the Summer Redneck Games in Texas, you can do all that and win prizes.

79. Instead of dinky little toilet bowls, the Scottish hurl 175-pound (80-kilogram) pillars into the air. The goal of the caber toss is to flip the 19-foot-6 (or 6 meters) long pole and make its top-end land as flat on the ground as possible.

80. In the noble Japanese sport of bo-taoshi ("pole toppling"), 2 teams of 150 players fight to get on top of each other team's huge 30-foot (9-meter) tall pole while keeping their own pole erect —don't laugh. For each side, 75 players stay on the defensive by huddling together to keep their bo stable, while the other 75 go on the offensive to bring down the other team's bo by climbing on top of the opposition. The absolute chaos that ensues can only be described as "capture the flag meets the zombie apocalypse." It gets pretty wild.

Chapter 10

Random Facts That Don't Fit In

Well, guys, there isn't much to say here. This chapter has no rhyme or reason. It's just a collection of amusing facts that I felt like putting here because there isn't enough space in the other chapters or the trivia is too random. They're misfits, like you and I.

***

1. Swiss people hate PowerPoint presentations so much that they actually started an Anti-PowerPoint Party. The APP posits that these unholy presentations have cost the country of Switzerland 2.1 billion francs ($2.3 billion) in damages. The solution? The good ol' paper flip chart.

2. The ancient founders of Switzerland were the Helvetii people. And that is what inspired the Helvetica font.

3. Comic Sans is the world's most hated font. Why? Because it's considered tasteless and immature. Even its inventor, Vincent Connare, said he hates it, admitting that he only used it once to file a complaint.

4. Bubble wrap was first sold as wallpaper. Engineers Alfred W. Fielding and Marc Chavannes managed to trap air between two plastic sheets, and after some time, it dawned on them that their air sandwich could be used to safely package fragile items. Their first major customer was the IBM tech corporation. Needless to say, they made a killing.

5. Well, actually... Paper bags are more harmful to the environment than plastic bags. Paper bags produce 70% more pollutants, require 4 times more energy to manufacture, and break down at a much slower rate. Eco-friendly alternatives are bags made of hemp or cotton canvas.

6. Some Ikea locations use mushrooms to package their products. Specifically, they use MycoComposite, a mycelium compound made of the white fuzz you see on moldy bread and spoiled strawberries, to create a resilient plastic substitute.

7. According to Facebook's statistics, more couples break up in the 2 weeks before Christmas and in the spring than any other time of the year.

8. A man once broke into Eminem's Detroit home, fixed himself a PB&J, and just left. He didn't take anything with him, not even his half-eaten sandwich. The culprit returned sometime later and stole just about everything except the furniture. He didn't make another PB&J the second time around.

9. The electric chair was invented by a dentist. Alfred Porter Southwick, in the late 1800s. After witnessing an inebriated gentleman stumble onto a power generator and get electrocuted, Southwick got the idea for his new device of human demise. His hope was that it would be used as a more humane method of execution than hanging.

10. Alfred Hitchcock, the director of *The Birds*, was terrified of eggs. In the words of the late ovophobe, "They revolt me. That white round thing without any holes, and when you break it, inside there's that yellow thing, round, without any holes... Blood is jolly, red. But egg yolk is yellow, revolting. I've never tasted it."

11. 144 of something is called a gross. For example, 12 dozen eggs is a gross of eggs.

12. A baker's dozen is 13. To avoid getting fined and flogged —or worse— for being accused of shortchanging their customers, medieval British bakers would throw in an extra loaf of bread as a precaution.

13. A fortnight is 2 weeks. More specifically, it's the contraction of "fourteen nights." Before you ask, no, I haven't played the game, and I never will.

14. A googol is a unit of measurement. It's written as a 1 followed by 100 zeroes. Beyond that is a googolplex, a number so ridiculously huge that it can't even be written. The headquarters of our algorithmic overlord Google is called the Googleplex.

15. If you are riding your donkey, then someone throws a rock at you, and you fall off, you are quite literally stoned off your ass.

16. People in vintage photos from the 1800s never smiled because they literally couldn't. It would take hours for cameras to get good exposure (for light to enter) and snap a picture back then. They were so slow that the people being photographed had to wear back braces to keep still, lest they risk a blurry photo and need to do it all over again.

17. A common trend around the late 1800s and early 1900s was for people to take photographs with dead people. The deceased would often be photographed sitting or lying down with their eyes wide open. Post-mortem photography was a way for family members to take one last photo before parting with their loved ones forever.

18. If there's a death on board, flight attendants will calmly carry the body to an empty row of seats and put a blanket over it but leave the head exposed —Why? I don't know— and keep the stiff hidden there until the plane lands. It's not always possible to land immediately, so you could be flying with a corpse and not know it.

19. It's very common for airplanes to collide with flying birds, so dead chickens are launched at them through a cannon to test the strength of the airplane's windshields before flying. This bizarre experiment is called the "bird strike test."

20. By removing a single olive from the passengers' inflight salads in the 1980s, American Airlines has saved $40,000 in expenses every year.

21. Commercial airline pilots and co-pilots never eat the same meal. That way, if the pilot gets food poisoning, the co-pilot can take over and avoid canceling the flight. Airline pilots are severely overworked and often exploited. Many of them doze off while flying.

22. The United States' TSA (Transportation Security Administration) has its own official Instagram page that showcases all the weird things it has confiscated over the years... You're welcome.

23. In August 2011, at the Miami International Airport, a man was caught with several snakes in his trousers and turtles stuffed into his pantyhose... He got greedy. If he settled for 1 trouser snake and 2 turtles, he could've pulled it off.

24. The following year at the Miami International Airport again, a man was caught smuggling a small aquarium's worth of live animals. Over 160 live tropical fish, eels, and other sea creatures hidden in a checked bag filled with seawater were confiscated. The smuggler planned to travel to Venezuela and sell it for a pretty Bolivar.

25. In April 2014, a woman brought an 8.5 in (22 centimeters) knife wrapped inside an enchilada as carry-on luggage. After discovering the weapon, the TSA let her board the plane and bring it with her.

26. Visitors at the Smuggler's Inn, located on the US-Canada border, are given night vision goggles to spot and denounce illegal trespassers.

27. Hotels in New Orleans grease the support beams of their balconies so drunk tourists don't try to climb them during Mardi Gras ("Fat Tuesday"). It started as a practical way to avoid a lawsuit but somehow became a new tradition and competition in which participants slather the poles with grease and rub themselves on them in the most suggestive ways they can think of. Like most things in Mardi Gras, it gets pretty wild.

28. As the name implies, the Aurora Ice Hotel in Alaska was made of ice. Everything from its walls to its ceilings, to its beds, to even its martini glasses was ice. It was closed down because it was unsafe, not because it was a slipping hazard but because it was considered a fire hazard for not having any fire alarms installed.

29. Coca-Cola basically created Santa Claus. The concept of St. Nick as a portly man with a white beard wearing red-and-white clothes was fabricated by Coca-Cola. It's no coincidence that both Coke's and Claus' signature colors are red and white.

30. Barbie the doll's real name is Barbara Millicent Roberts. This all-American girl was "born" in Willows, Wisconsin, on March 9, 1959.

31. Ken Masters, from *Street Fighter*, didn't have a surname at first. He got his "Masters" because Capcom needed to distinguish their character's action figures from the Barbie franchise's Ken dolls.

32. Highschool anime, fried chicken, and pretty boys, if you, like many people, have wondered how you could enjoy these three specific things at the same time, then consider your prayers answered. *I Love You, Colonel Sanders! A Finger Lickin' Good Dating Simulator* is a game licensed by KFC itself in which you can gain the affection of a younger, even more handsome Col. Sanders while working hard at an anime culinary school to create the perfect fried poultry. And as if it couldn't get any better, your homeroom teacher is a talking corgi named "Sprinkles." No need to pinch yourself; it's 100% real.

33. Jon Steinbeck's dog actually ate his homework. Soon after writing his first draft of Of *Mice and Men*, his pooch chewed it up. Steinbeck was thankful and quipped, "I was pretty mad, but the poor fellow may have been acting critically."

34. Pope Francis used to be a bouncer at nightclubs. During his doorman days, he went by the name Jorge Mario Bergoglio. It's common to take on a new name when assuming the papacy, usually a previous pope's namesake.

35. An art collector once paid $10,000 for an invisible sculpture. James Franco held a "non-visible" art exhibit in which he put for sale a masterpiece of abstract art that he described as an "endless tanks of oxygen." And some fancy pants who never once got dirt under their finely manicured nails wasted 10 grand on literal thin air... A lot of hungry mouths could have been fed with that money.

36. Type "Florida Man" plus your birthday into your favorite search engine, and you will almost always find some kind of strange news involving the Sunshine State.

37. Computer programmer Maneesh Sethi paid a woman to sit beside him and slap him every time he checked his Facebook during work to boost productivity... Now there's a business idea!

38. Cookie Monster's real name is Sid... It doesn't start with "C," but that's good enough for me. If Cookie Monster were British, do you think they would call him "Biscuit Monster" and make him sing "B is for biscuit?" Never mind the biscuits.

39. The gender-neutral term for "nieces" and "nephews" is "niblings." But if they're not born yet, they're your nieflings.

40. The Secret Intelligence Service (British CIA, basically) hacked into Al-Qaeda's network and replaced their bomb instructions with a cupcake recipe... Sweet.

Remember to Leave a Quick Review

It's a well-known fact that books with more reviews do better on the market. Sadly, only 1 out of every 100 readers —just 1%— leave reviews, even if they love the book. A writer is only as great as his readers. Without your help, small-time authors like myself can't hope to compete against million-dollar publishing companies or keep writing awesome books for you to read.

So, if you enjoyed *1000 Fun Facts for Immature Adults Vol. 1* and would like to see more like it, I would be incredibly grateful if you could take a few quick seconds to write a brief review on Amazon, even if it's just a few sentences. It won't take long. Trust me, all I do is spit facts. And you read all 1000 of them. Great job, by the way.

Please go to Amazon to leave your review or scan this QR code:

If you're up for it, kindly include a picture of your book. It can be the cover, your favorite page, fact, drawing, or just your sexy self holding the book. You'll make us happy either way.

Momoko and I love hearing from our readers, and we personally read every single review.

Thank you! Arigatou! Your support makes passion projects like this possible.

Conclusion

Thank you for reading *1000 Fun Facts for Immature Adults Vol. 1.* You're awesome! Seriously. Almost nobody reads books from cover to cover these days.

We hope you had a great time learning new and unusual facts. Most importantly, we hope our little passion project helped reignite that childhood sense of wonder and wild curiosity within you. Never listen to people who tell you to "grow up."

So, what's next? You can count on Vol. 2 coming out eventually, but we have a Japan factbook in the works right now. If you haven't been to Japan yet, go. Japan is surprisingly affordable for tourists. Tokyo, Kyoto, and Osaka are great, but you can't forget about Hiroshima, Nagasaki, Nagoya, and Sapporo. They're all stunning places with their own unique feel.

Wanna Get Connected?

Join the Fun Facts for Immature Adults Facebook group at:

https://www.facebook.com/groups/itsnotbs

If you'd like to get in touch with me directly, hit me up at:

bryanspektor@itsnotbs.com

What was your favorite chapter? What kind of trivia would you like to read about next? Let me know.

Would you like to commission artwork from Momoko? Send an email with the subject line "Not you, Bryan" You know she's good. You've seen what she can do.

Welp, that's all, folks. If you haven't already, remember to pick up your 150 FREE bonus facts on your way out.

150 Mind-Blowing Bonus Facts

Don't Forget Your Three FREE Books!

If *1000 Fun Facts for Immature Adults* is the approved theatrical release, then bonus chapters one and two are the unrated deleted scenes. The facts within them might be too real for general audiences and are reserved only for the most curious of cats with a few extra lives to spare. The third bonus is the post-credits scene to lighten up the mood.

Get your three FREE books when you join Bryan Spektor's spectacular, factacular newsletter at www.itsnotbs.com (no apostrophe needed). Or simply scan the QR code below for instant access:

Just So You Know I'm Not Making This Stuff Up...

5 Fascinating Facts About the Hawaiian Language. (2019, June 4). Trip Trivia. https://www.t riptrivia.com/5-fascinating-facts-about-the-hawaiian-language/XphLiNfEsAAGy_E0

7 Cool Facts about Cactus You Didn't Know About! (2021, May 11). Succulent Alley. https://su cculentalley.com/cool-facts-about-cactus/

7 crazy things people smuggle on planes. (n.d.). Wanderlust. Retrieved March 19, 2021, from https://www.wanderlust.co.uk/content/7-crazy-things-people-smuggle-on-planes/

8 Shocking Facts About Electric Eels. (n.d.). Treehugger. https://www.treehugger.com/shock ing-facts-about-electric-eels-4863966

10 Weird Laws in Italy |Funny Ways to Get Fined | LivItaly. (2017, October 13). LivItaly Tours. https://www.livitaly.com/weird-laws-funny-italian-laws/

15 Things You Didn't Know About John F. Kennedy. (2017, January 26). Goliath. https://www .goliath.com/random/15-things-you-didnt-know-about-john-f-kennedy/

30 Interesting Facts About Baseball. (2020, October 16). Kickass Facts. https://www.kickassf acts.com/30-kickass-interesting-facts-about-baseball/

35 Interesting Hotels and Motels Around the World. (2021, August 24). Fact Republic. https:/ /factrepublic.com/35-interesting-hotels-and-motels-around-the-world/

82 facts about Hawaii (bet you never heard of Hawaii fact 32). (2021, July 7). CosmopoliClan. https://cosmopoliclan.com/travel-with-kids/inspiration/facts-about-hawaii/

100 Greatest Animal Facts That Will Blow Your Mind. (2021, February 18). Fact Animal. http s://factanimal.com/animal-facts/

A.A.S. Team. (2021, August 6). The Countries With the Most Official Languages and How They Translate. Ad Astra, Inc. https://ad-astrainc.com/2021/08/the-countries-with-the-most-offi cial-languages-and-how-they-translate/

Abrego, N., & Feldman, G. (2021, January 8). 23 Amazing Facts About Dogs You Probably Didn't Know - Veterinarian in Encinitas, CA. The Drake Center For Veterinary Care. https://www.thedrakecenter.com/services/dogs/blog/23-amazing-facts-about-dogs-y ou-probably-didnt-know

Ajinomoto. (n.d.-a). What is MSG and how is it made? | Monosodium Glutamate (MSG). https://www.ajinomoto.com/msg/what-is-msg-and-how-is-it-made

Ajinomoto. (n.d.-b). What is umami? 5 facts about umami | Everything about umami | Umami Global Website. https://www.ajinomoto.com/aboutus/umami/5-facts

Alexander, C. (2020, August 17). 24 Levelled-Up Facts About Super Mario & Friends. Factinate. https://www.factinate.com/things/24-levelled-facts-super-mario-friends/

Alexander, D. (2020, October 18). 13 Out of This World Facts About Spacesuits That You Should Know. Interesting Engineering. https://interestingengineering.com/13-out-of-this-world-facts-about-spacesuits-that-you-should-know

American Gem Society. (2021, June 10). Diamond Facts for Kids and Adults. https://www.americangemsociety.org/diamond-facts-for-kids-and-adults/

American Museum of Natural History. (n.d.). Tyrannosaurus rex. AMNH. Retrieved May 7, 2021, from https://www.amnh.org/dinosaurs/tyrannosaurus-rex

Andrew, E. (2019, March 11). Could T. Rex Really Only See You If You Moved? IFLScience. https://www.iflscience.com/plants-and-animals/could-t-rex-really-only-see-you-if-you-moved/

Andrews, E. (2018, September 1). 8 Reasons It Wasn't Easy Being Spartan. History. https://www.history.com/news/8-reasons-it-wasnt-easy-being-spartan

Andrews, E. (2021, April 26). 10 Little-Known Facts About Cleopatra. History https://www.history.com/news/10-little-known-facts-about-cleopatra

Andrus, J. (2019, March 12). Fun Fact Friday! Some interesting facts about ears and hearing. Hearing Institute Atlantic. https://hearinginstitute.ca/fun-fact-friday-some-interesting-facts-about-ears-and-hearing/

Antidote. (2017, December 1). BC and AD, BCE and CE: What's the Difference? https://www.antidote.info/en/blog/reports/bc-and-ad-bce-and-ce-whats-difference

Are Chickens Really The Closest Descendants Of T-Rex? (2017, December 13). Earth Buddies. https://earthbuddies.net/are-chickens-really-the-closest-descendants-of-t-rex

Are Raindrops Shaped Like Teardrops? (n.d.). USGS. https://www.usgs.gov/special-topic/water-science-school/science/are-raindrops-shaped-teardrops

Atkinson, O. (2017, August 30). 30 Weird Phobias You Never Knew Existed. Urban List. https://www.theurbanlist.com/a-list/30-weird-phobias-you-never-knew-existed

Avakian, T. (2015, August 6). 16 odd things that are illegal in Singapore. Business Insider Australia. https://www.businessinsider.com.au/things-that-are-illegal-in-singapore-2015-7

Barker, E. (2020, March 19). Outkast: 50 Incredibly Geeky Facts. NME. https://www.nme.co m/photos/outkast-50-incredibly-geeky-facts-1421504

Bassi, I. (2017, September 5). 27 Facts That Will Make You Appreciate "Jurassic Park" Even More. BuzzFeed. https://www.buzzfeed.com/ishabassi/jurassic-times-call-for-jurassic-measures

Black, A. (2019, November 5). What You Don't Know About Ketchup (It's Not Just America's Favorite Condiment). Taste of Home. https://www.tasteofhome.com/article/10-crazy-facts-a bout-ketchup/

Bryan, M. (2021, June 9). Marilyn Monroe Facts. Facts.Net. https://facts.net/history/people/m arilyn-monroe-facts/

Brodwin, E. (2016, April 27). 14 seemingly harmless things you eat, drink, and use all the time that could kill you. Business Insider. https://www.businessinsider.com/things-that-seem-h armless-but-can-kill-2016-4?international=true&r=US&IR=T

Buchholz, K. (2020, September 10). Oodles of Noodles: Instant Noodle Consumption Around the World. Statista Infographics. https://www.statista.com/chart/22865/instant-noodle-con sumption-by-country/

Burke, M. (2020a, September 3). 40 Whimsical Facts About Studio Ghibli. Factinate. https://www.factinate.com/things/40-whimsical-facts-studio-ghiblii/

Burke, M. (2020b, November 13). Epic Facts About The Lord Of The Rings. Factinate. https://www.factinate.com/things/44-epic-facts-lord-rings/

Burke, M. (2020c, November 13). Mind-Blowing Facts About The Human Body. Factinate. https://www.factinate.com/things/50-interesting-facts-human-body/

Burke, M. (2020d, November 13). Neuron-Popping Facts About The Human Brain. Factinate. https://www.factinate.com/things/32-neuron-popping-facts-human-brain/

Burke, M. (2020e, November 13). Out-Of-This-World Facts About Space. Factinate. https://w ww.factinate.com/places/40-world-facts-space/

Burke, M. (2020f, November 27). 54 Golden Facts About The Aztec Civilization. Factinate. https://www.factinate.com/people/28-facts-aztecs-civilization/

Burke, M. (2020g, December 18). 54 Facts about Eminem That'll Make You Lose Yourself. Factinate. https://www.factinate.com/people/54-facts-eminem/

C. (2021, February 23). Pina Colada Origin - History and Facts About The Popular Tropical Cocktail. Always the Holidays. https://alwaystheholidays.com/pina-colada-origin-history/

Cactus Facts - 15 Interesting Facts About Cactus. (2018, July 15). Kickass Facts. https://www.kickassfacts.com/cactus-facts/

Cape Town Diamond Museum. (2017, May 17). Top 10 facts about diamonds you didn't know. https://www.capetowndiamondmuseum.org/blog/2017/03/top-10-facts-about-diamonds-you-didnt-know/

Carson, J. (2020, August 19). 21 Facts About the Aztec Empire. History Hit. https://www.historyhit.com/facts-about-aztec-empire/

Castro, J. (2014, March 17). 11 Surprising Facts About the Skeletal System. Live Science. https://www.livescience.com/44137-skeletal-system-surprising-facts.html

Castro, J. (2016, March 18). Triceratops: Facts About the Three-Horned Dinosaur. Livescience.Com. https://www.livescience.com/24011-triceratops-facts.html

Castro, J. (2017, October 17). Tyrannosaurus Rex: King of the Dinosaurs. Livescience.Com. https://www.livescience.com/23868-tyrannosaurus-rex-facts.html

Cellania, M. (2015, February 24). 15 Fascinating Flamingo Facts. Mental Floss. https://www.mentalfloss.com/article/61853/15-fascinating-flamingo-facts

Chaneac, S. (2021, February 19). 15 interesting facts about Cambodia. Nomadic Boys. https://nomadicboys.com/interesting-facts-about-cambodia/

Chase, C. (2019, August 22). 101 incredible sports facts that will blow your mind. For The Win. https://ftw.usatoday.com/2015/04/best-101-sports-facts-trivia-crazy-amazing-incredible-babe-ruth-michael-phelps-michael-jordan

Chetty, A. (2021, February 9). 27 Amazing Facts About Wild Animals That Will Surprise You. The Carousel. https://thecarousel.com/environment/27-amazing-facts-about-wild-animals/

Chicken Facts. (2020, December 22). Facts.Net. https://facts.net/nature/animals/chicken-facts/

Christina, C. (2019, January 8). "Star Wars" cast: 25 greatest untold stories. CBS News. https://www.cbsnews.com/pictures/star-wars-cast-greatest-untold-stories/

Cleal, S. (2021, February 8). 22 Fascinating Facts About Space That Gave Me A Healthy Dose Of Existential Dread. BuzzFeed. https://www.buzzfeed.com/sam_cleal/fascinating-facts-about-space

Climans, K. (2020, August 17). 42 Epic Facts About The Battle Of Thermopylae And The 300 Spartans. Factinate. https://www.factinate.com/things/42-epic-facts-battle-thermopylae-300-spartans/

Climans, K. (2020b, August 17). 42 Swashbuckling Facts About The Pirates Of The Caribbean Movies. Factinate. https://www.factinate.com/things/42-swashbuckling-facts-pirates-caribbean-movies/

Cohen, J. (2018, September 4). 10 Things You May Not Know About the Vikings. History. https://www.history.com/news/10-things-you-may-not-know-about-the-vikings

Corrigan, D. (2019, July 24). Interesting Facts About Spain: Food and Wine. TripSavvy. https://www.tripsavvy.com/spanish-food-and-wine-1643209

Crow, S. (2019, December 24). 45 Amazing Facts About Airplanes That Will Make Your Mind Soar. Best Life. https://bestlifeonline.com/airplane-facts/

D. (2020, September 14). 50 Creepy, Strange and Gross Facts About Death. Rebel Circus. https://therebelcircus.com/news/50-creepy-strange-and-gross-facts-about-death/

Daniel, A. (2019, December 9). 25 Health Myths You Need To Stop Believing. Best Life. https://bestlifeonline.com/health-myths/

Das, B. (2020, April 25). 15 Most Interesting Facts About Sherlock Holmes. RankRed. https://www.rankred.com/interesting-facts-about-sherlock-holmes/

Davies, E. (2016, August 10). Earth's saltiest place makes the Dead Sea look like tapwater. BBC Earth. http://www.bbc.com/earth/story/20160809-earths-saltiest-place-makes-the-dead-sea-look-like-tapwater

Davies, N. (2020, May 18). Guide to cuckoos: where to see in Britain and why the species is in decline. Countryfile. https://www.countryfile.com/wildlife/where-to-see/guide-to-cuckoos-where-to-see-in-britain-and-why-the-species-is-in-decline/

Delbert, C. (2020, December 4). 50 fascinating facts about the internet. Stacker. https://stacker.com/stories/5205/50-fascinating-facts-about-internet

Dictionary.com. (2021, January 19). The Original Memes (Before Memes). https://www.dictionary.com/e/the-original-memes-before-memes-listicle/

DiSilvestro, A. (2017, September 1). From customs to tradition: 9 things you didn't know about Cuban culture. Volunteer Vacations | Discover Corps. https://discovercorps.com/blog/customs-tradition-cuban-culture/

Dr. Dre Facts. (2019, April 29). Celebrity Fun Facts. https://www.celebrityfunfacts.com/dr-dre/

Drapkin, J. (2008, April 18). LBJ: The President Who Marked His Territory. Mental Floss. http s://www.mentalfloss.com/article/18463/lbj-president-who-marked-his-territory

Dreher, B., & Jones, M. (2021, March 29). 10 Weird Facts About Rain. Reader's Digest. https:// www.rd.com/list/rain-facts/

Dying Matters. (2021, February 25). Interesting facts about dying. https://www.dyingmatter s.org/page/interesting-facts-about-dying

Eaton, V. (2017, November 9). 8 Oldest Sports in the World. Oldest.Org. https://www.oldest. org/sports/sports/

Editorial Staff. (2021a, May 10). 50 Interesting Facts About Golf. The Fact File. https://thefactf ile.org/golf-facts/

Editorial Staff. (2021b, June 24). 50 Interesting Facts About Michael Phelps. The Fact File. https://thefactfile.org/michael-phelps-facts/

EHL Insights. (n.d.). Fun Facts About Singapore. Hospitality Insights. Retrieved July 14, 2021, from https://hospitalityinsights.ehl.edu/fun-facts-singapore

Euditeankit Singh. (2019, October 19). how to hypnotize a chicken with one line [Video]. YouTube. https://www.youtube.com/watch?v=8Yo2UkL-n_Q

Eschner, K. (2017, May 12). Apple Pie Is Not All That American. Smithsonian Magazine. https ://www.smithsonianmag.com/smart-news/why-apple-pie-linked-america-180963157/

Expert Photography. (2021, May 18). 25 Awesome Photography Facts We Bet You Didn't Know! https://expertphotography.com/photography-facts/

Fact Fiend. (2020, September 11). Eminem's Favourite Book Is The Dictionary (Song Lyrics We Dislike) [Video]. YouTube. https://www.youtube.com/watch?v=zjwvg8fj_nA

Facts Legend. (2021a, April 9). 40 Awesome Pineapple Facts for Fruit Lovers. https://factsleg end.org/40-awesome-pineapple-facts-for-fruit-lovers/

Facts Legend. (2021b, April 20). 60 Awesome Garlic Facts You Must Know. https://factslegen d.org/60-awesome-garlic-facts-you-must-know/

Facts Legend. (2021c, April 29). 20 Tempting Avocado Facts: Here's a List You'll Love! https:/ /factslegend.org/20-avocado-facts-you-should-know/

Facts Legend. (2021d, April 29). 20 Tempting Avocado Facts: Here's a List You'll Love! https://factslegend.org/20-avocado-facts-you-should-know/

Facts Legend. (2021e, June 15). 30 Interesting Human Teeth Facts. https://factslegend.org/30-interesting-human-teeth-facts/

Fantozzi, J. (2020, August 3). 30 food facts that will blow your mind. Insider. https://www.insider.com/amazing-food-facts-2017-12

Fater, L. (2019, August 1). The Pirate Who Penned the First English-Language Guacamole Recipe. Atlas Obscura. https://www.atlasobscura.com/articles/first-food-writer

Felthousen-Post, C. (2019, May 25). Italian Food Before the Tomato. History Daily. https://historydaily.org/italian-food-before-the-tomato

Funk, R. (n.d.). 15 Things You Might Not Know About the Dead Sea. Great Value Vacations. https://www.greatvaluevacations.com/travel-inspiration/dead-sea-facts

G., R. (2019, December 9). 20 Surprising Facts Fans Choose To Ignore About Eminem. TheThings. https://www.thethings.com/20-surprising-facts-fans-choose-to-ignore-about-eminem/

G., R. (2020, April 22). 17 Years Of Get Rich Or Die Tryin': Facts About 50 Cent's Breakthrough Album. TheThings. https://www.thethings.com/get-rich-or-die-tryin-50-cent-breakthrough-album-facts-rapper/

G., R. (2020, September 9). 10 Things You Didn't Know About Eminem's Friendship With Dr. Dre. TheThings. https://www.thethings.com/eminem-dr-dre-friendship-trivia-facts/

Gane, T. (2021, May 26). 50 Facts About America That Most Americans Don't Know. Reader's Digest. https://www.rd.com/list/america-fascinating-facts/

George Herald. (2018, September 17). Hurricane, Cyclone, Typhoon, Tornado – What's The Difference? https://www.georgeherald.com/News/Article/International/hurricane-cyclone-typhoon-tornado-what-s-the-difference-201809170355

Glubiak, E. (n.d.). 11 Facts About Buffalo Wings You Probably Didn't Know. Spoon University. https://spoonuniversity.com/lifestyle/buffalo-wing-facts-you-did-not-know

Goldhammer, Z. (2020, October 16). Why Americans Call Turkey 'Turkey.' The Atlantic. https://www.theatlantic.com/international/archive/2014/11/why-americans-call-turkey-turkey/383225/

Gomes, H. (2021, July 16). Gripping Facts About Wrestling. Factinate. https://www.factinate.com/things/42-gripping-facts-wrestling/

Goodhart, B. (2021, July 22). The ten weirdest events in Olympic Games history: from pistol duelling to poodle clipping. British GQ. https://www.gq-magazine.co.uk/lifestyle/article/olympic-games-weirdest-events

Gottesman, B. (2018, September 2). 10 Surprising Facts About J.R.R. Tolkien. Mental Floss. https://www.mentalfloss.com/article/59736/10-things-you-might-not-know-about-jrr-tolkien

Great Big Story. (2018, February 7). Have a Seat at the Oldest Restaurant in the World [Video]. YouTube. https://www.youtube.com/watch?v=c24xTGTaTNI

Greater Roadrunner Overview, All About Birds, Cornell Lab of Ornithology. (n.d.). All About Birds. https://www.allaboutbirds.org/guide/Greater_Roadrunner/overview

Greenwood, C. (2014, November 26). 101 Dalmatians: 7 things you never knew about the doggy Disney classic. Mirror. https://www.mirror.co.uk/tv/tv-news/101-dalmatians-7-things-you-3427936

Griffiths, J. (2017, February 10). 15 Shocking Things You Didn't Know About The Street Fighter Franchise. The Gamer. https://www.thegamer.com/15-shocking-things-you-didnt-know-about-the-street-fighter-franchise/

Guadua Bamboo. (n.d.). Guadua Bamboo. https://www.guaduabamboo.com/

Guinness World Records. (2012, September 16). Heaviest weight pulled with the tongue (female). https://www.guinnessworldrecords.com/world-records/109104-heaviest-weight-pulled-with-the-tongue-female

Guinness World Records. (2014, September 20). Most teeth in a mouth. https://www.guinnessworldrecords.com/world-records/most-teeth-in-a-mouth

Guinness World Records. (n.d.). Longest baby. Retrieved April 16, 2021, from https://www.guinnessworldrecords.com/world-records/longest-baby

Guinness World Records. (n.d.). Oldest amusement park in operation. https://www.guinnessworldrecords.com/world-records/oldest-amusement-park-in-operation

Guinness World Records. (2018, September 14). Most bites taken from three apples whilst juggling in one minute. https://www.guinnessworldrecords.com/world-records/104419-most-bites-taken-from-three-apples-whilst-juggling-in-one-minute

Guinness World Records. (2021, June 18). The largest mouth gape! - Guinness World Records [Video]. YouTube. https://www.youtube.com/watch?v=9ZrME1aVyaM

Gupta, M. S. (2021, July 27). 14 interesting facts you probably never knew about the Olympic Games. Lifestyle Asia Singapore. https://www.lifestyleasia.com/sg/culture/events/14-interesting-facts-you-probably-never-knew-about-the-olympic-games/

Hartley, S. (2020, February 15). 17 hippopotamus facts in honor of National Hippo Day. Napa Valley Register. https://napavalleyregister.com/lifestyles/17-hippopotamus-facts-in-honor-of-national-hippo-day/collection_94cd5956-4ed1-11ea-ad98-c360170ab888.html

Hawkins, A. (2014, October 6). 11 Apple Facts You Probably Didn't Know. Good Housekeeping. https://www.goodhousekeeping.com/health/diet-nutrition/a25849/apple-facts/

Heimbuch, J. (2021, March 25). 13 Fascinating Facts About Elephants. Treehugger. https://www.treehugger.com/facts-change-way-see-elephants-4869315

Hewitt, D. G. (2019, November 11). 40 Facts about the Gladiators of Ancient Rome. HistoryCollection. https://historycollection.com/40-facts-about-the-gladiators-of-ancient-rome/

Hill, S. (2021, April 20). 10 Most Powerful Animal Bites on the Planet. Field & Stream. https://www.fieldandstream.com/10-most-powerful-animal-bites-on-planet/

History.com Editors. (2021, April 16). History of Thanksgiving. History. https://www.history.com/topics/thanksgiving/history-of-thanksgiving

Hoekstra, K. (2021, July 5). Sir Arthur Conan Doyle: 10 Facts About Sherlock Holmes's Creator. History Hit. https://www.historyhit.com/sir-arthur-conan-doyle-facts-about-sherlock-holmes-creator/

Holland, L. (2012, October 19). 50 Things You Didn't Know About James Bond. NME. https://www.nme.com/blogs/the-movies-blog/50-things-you-didnt-know-about-james-bond-759514

Holmes, M. (2021, January 27). The Corpse Flower: Description, Life Cycle, Facts, and More. Treehugger. https://www.treehugger.com/corpse-flower-amorphophallus-titanum-5095935

Houser, K. (2017, November 10). Eight "Facts" about the Human Body Debunked by Science. Futurism. https://futurism.com/neoscope/human-body-myths

Howard, B. C. (2014, July 23). 11 Surprising Facts and Myths About Microwave Ovens. MSN. https://www.msn.com/en-us/news/other/11-surprising-facts-and-myths-about-microwave-ovens/ar-AA3dhCL

Hussein, J. (2019, May 29). 50 Things You Don't Know About Chocolate. Eat This Not That. https://www.eatthis.com/chocolate-facts/

Hutchinson, S. (2019, May 4). 65 Facts About the Star Wars Universe. Mental Floss. https://www.mentalfloss.com/article/79553/60-facts-about-star-wars-universe-star-wars-day

Hyenas Cooperate, Problem-solve Better Than Primates. (2009, September 29). ScienceDaily. https://www.sciencedaily.com/releases/2009/09/090928131032.htm

I Love You, Colonel Sanders! A Finger Lickin' Good Dating Simulator. (2021, July 20). Know Your Meme. https://knowyourmeme.com/memes/subcultures/i-love-you-colonel-sanders-a-finger-lickin-good-dating-simulator

International Rhino Foundation. (2020, November 3). Rhino Species. https://rhinos.org/about-rhinos/rhino-species/

Israelsen, J. (2020, January 10). 43 Fresh Rap and Hip Hop Facts. Fact Retriever. https://www.factretriever.com/hip-hop-facts

Italy's free wine fountain, and other bizarre Italian facts. (2020, June 12). Trafalgar. https://www.trafalgar.com/real-word/fun-facts-about-italy/

Jacques, R. (2017, December 7). 10 Things About Instant Ramen You'll Be Embarrassed You Never Knew. HuffPost. https://www.huffpost.com/entry/ramen-facts_n_5784632

Jandreau, C. (n.d.). Fascinating Facts About Mushrooms That'll Blow Your Mind. Ranker. https://www.ranker.com/list/mushroom-facts/coy-jandreau

Julius Caesar Had Tamed Elephants Shipped From Italy To Calm His Men And Horses In Preparation For His Battles In North Africa. (2022, July 21). The Historian's Hut. https://thehistorianshut.com/2017/05/08/julius-caesar-had-tamed-elephants-shipped-from-italy-to-calm-his-men-and-horses-in-preparation-for-his-battles-in-north-africa/

Kariega Game Reserve. (n.d.). 10 Fascinating Facts About Hippos. https://www.kariega.co.za/blog/10-fascinating-facts-about-hippos

Kershner, E. (2020, July 31). Which Country Has The Most Lakes In The World? WorldAtlas. https://www.worldatlas.com/articles/which-country-has-the-most-lakes-in-the-world.html

Kiversal. (2018, August 13). 10 interesting facts about ears and hearing. Blog of Kiversal. https://blog.kiversal.com/en/10-facts-about-ears-and-hearing/

Klein, C. (2018, September 1). 10 Things You May Not Know About Christopher Columbus. History. https://www.history.com/news/10-things-you-may-not-know-about-christopher-columbus

Klein, C. (2020, December 18). 8 Things You May Not Know About the Real Colonel Sanders. History. https://www.history.com/news/8-facts-real-colonel-sanders-kfc

Kooser, A. (2016, October 18). 20 weirdest items confiscated by the TSA, in pictures. CNET. https://www.cnet.com/pictures/tsa-transportation-security-administration-banned-weird-items/18/

Kowinsky, J. (n.d.). Your Complete Guide to Mosasaurs. Fossil Guy. Retrieved May 11, 2021, from https://www.fossilguy.com/gallery/vert/reptile/mosasaur/index.htm#

LaMotte, S. C. (2019b, October 4). Bugs, rodent hair and poop: How much is legally allowed in the food you eat every day? CNN. https://edition.cnn.com/2019/10/04/health/insect-rodent-filth-in-food-wellness/index.html

Lapper, C. (2021, June 2). 30 surprising facts about Switzerland | Expatica guide to Switzerland. Expat Guide to Switzerland | Expatica. https://www.expatica.com/ch/moving/about/switzerland-facts-100041/

Larkin, B. (2020, September 10). 40 Facts So Funny They're Hard to Believe. Best Life. https://bestlifeonline.com/funniest-facts/

Lehnardt, K. (2019b, August 15). 58 Winning Football Facts. FactRetriever. https://www.factretriever.com/football-facts

Lehnardt, K. (2019c, September 9). 62 Interesting Wolf Facts. Fact Retriever. https://www.factretriever.com/wolves-facts

Lehnardt, K. (2019, November 21). 78 Interesting Snake Facts. FactRetriever. https://www.factretriever.com/snake-facts

Lehnardt, K. (2020, July 17). 26 Amazing Oak Tree Facts. Fact Retriever. https://www.factretriever.com/oak-tree-facts

Lenz, L. (2015, May 1). 12 Wild Facts About Hyenas. Mental Floss. https://www.mentalfloss.com/article/63455/12-wild-facts-about-hyenas

Lewis, K. (2018, December 15). 10 Wild And Crazy Facts About Ketchup. Listverse. https://listverse.com/2014/07/29/10-wild-and-crazy-facts-about-ketchup/

Love Big Island. (2021, May 17). Pineapples In Hawai'i: History, Facts, and Trivia. https://www.lovebigisland.com/quick-and-remarkable-facts-about-hawaii/pineapple/

Mancini, M. (2016a, May 26). 10 Colorful Facts About Cassowaries. Mental Floss. https://www.mentalfloss.com/article/80394/10-facts-about-cassowaries

Martini's law. (n.d.). TheFreeDictionary.Com. https://medical-dictionary.thefreedictionary.com/Martini%27s+law

Massabrook, N. (2022, May 18). Diddy's Different Names Through the Years: Puffy, P. Diddy and More. Us Weekly. https://www.usmagazine.com/celebrity-news/pictures/diddys-different-names-through-the-years-puffy-and-more/

Mauldin, D. (2019, July 18). Fans Can't Get Enough Of These Strange Sports. TieBreaker. https://www.tiebreaker.com/strange-sports/

McCaffery, J. (2021, March 29). 13 Things You Probably Never Knew About Salt. Reader's Digest. https://www.rd.com/list/facts-about-salt/

McLendon, R. (2021, April 1). 9 Interesting Facts About Wolves. Treehugger. https://www.treehugger.com/wolf-facts-5120321

McVean B.Sc., A. (2017, June 20). Is Himalayan Pink Salt Better For You? McGill Office for Science and Society. https://www.mcgill.ca/oss/article/health-and-nutrition-quackery-you-asked/himalayan-pink-salt

Mead, D. (2017, October 3). 50 Random MLB Facts You Never Knew. Bleacher Report. https://bleacherreport.com/articles/981899-50-random-mlb-facts-you-never-knew

Mendoran, S. (2021, February 19). A Comprehensive List of Animal Group Names. Owlcation - Education. https://owlcation.com/stem/collective-names-for-groups-of-animals

Mersereau, D. (2017, July 14). 10 Myths About Tornadoes Debunked. Mental Floss. https://www.mentalfloss.com/article/502747/10-myths-about-tornadoes-debunked

Miller, M. (2016, July 1). The Insanely Stupid Accident That Nearly Ruined Skyfall. Esquire. https://www.esquire.com/entertainment/movies/news/a46370/daniel-craig-skyfall-gloves/

Miller, L. (2018, September 5). 20 Crazy Details Behind Making Of The Chronicles Of Narnia Movies. Screen Rant. https://screenrant.com/chronicles-narnia-movies-behind-scenes-making-details-trivia/

Mohr, I. (2020, April 15). 50 Cent avoids drinking his own champagne in the club. Page Six. https://pagesix.com/2020/04/14/50-cent-avoids-drinking-his-own-champagne-in-the-club/

Moran, L. (2012, February 8). John F Kennedy bought 1,200 Cuban cigars hours before he ordered US trade embargo. Mail Online. https://www.dailymail.co.uk/news/article-209806 4/John-F-Kennedy-bought-1-200-Cuban-cigars-hours-ordered-US-trade-embargo.html

Mozley, S. (2002, May 21). Animal Nomenclature. North Carolina State University. https://pr ojects.ncsu.edu/cals/course/zo150/mozley/nomencla.html

MrBeast. (2020, February 29). I Ate A $70,000 Golden Pizza [Video]. YouTube. https://www. youtube.com/watch?v=F4Y3Pkn95GI

Myers, D. (2017, April 3). 10 things you didn't know about Nutella. Insider. https://www.insi der.com/facts-about-nutella-2017-4

N. (2021b, June 11). 34 Fun and Interesting Facts About Puerto Rico You Probably Didn't Know. GloboTreks. https://www.globotreks.com/destinations/puerto-rico/fun-interesting-f acts-about-puerto-rico/

N. (2021c, June 18). 32 Interesting Switzerland Facts You Should Know. The World Pursuit. https://theworldpursuit.com/facts-about-switzerland/

N. (2021d, June 18). 36 Fun Facts About Spain You Should Know! The World Pursuit. https://t heworldpursuit.com/facts-about-spain/

NASA. (n.d.). Facts About Spacesuits and Spacewalking. Retrieved August 21, 2021, from http s://www.nasa.gov/audience/foreducators/spacesuits/facts/index.html

Nag, O. S. (2019, August 29). Top 10 Interesting Facts About Pakistan. WorldAtlas. https://ww w.worldatlas.com/articles/top-10-interesting-facts-about-pakistan.html

Nahigyan, P. (2021, April 6). Facts About Ancient Roman Emperors That Made Us Say "Really?" Ranker. https://www.ranker.com/list/whoa-roman-emperor-facts/pierce-nahigyan

Nargi, L. (2021, May 25). 20 Cool Facts About Space We Bet You Didn't Know. Reader's Digest. https://www.rd.com/list/space-travel-facts/

National Oceanic and Atmospheric Administration. (2020, August 19). 5 striking facts versus myths about lightning you should know | National Oceanic and Atmospheric Administration. NOAA. https://www.noaa.gov/stories/5-striking-facts-versus-myths-about-lightning-you-s hould-know

Nazario, M. (2017, April 28). 7 Things You Never Knew About Cranberries. Spoon University. https://spoonuniversity.com/lifestyle/cranberries-fun-facts

Noor, P. (2020, January 30). Danger! "Avocado hand" is on the rise – here's how to stay safe this Super Bowl. The Guardian. https://www.theguardian.com/food/2020/jan/30/avocado-hand-super-bowl-sunday

North Seattle Dental. (2019, March 11). 7 Foods That Torment Your Teeth. https://northseattledental.com/7-foods-that-torment-your-teeth/

Nowak, C. (2021, August 16). 25 Science Facts You Never Learned in School. Reader's Digest. https://www.rd.com/list/science-facts-never-learned/

Ocean Spray. (n.d.). Our Cranberry Harvest. https://www.oceanspray.com/en/Our-Story/About-the-Harvest

Oconnel, R. (2017, April 11). 11 Wild Facts About Dingoes. Mental Floss. https://www.mentalfloss.com/article/78190/11-wild-facts-about-dingoes

Ojala, A. (2021, June 4). 32 Mind Boggling Facts About the Internet. LifeHacks. https://lifehacks.io/facts-about-the-internet/

Old Farmer's Almanac. (n.d.). Where did the names of the days of the week come from? https://www.almanac.com/fact/where-did-the-names-of-the-days

OneKindPlanet. (n.d.-b). Red Fox. https://onekindplanet.org/animal/fox-red/

OneKindPlanet. (n.d.). Hippopotamus. https://onekindplanet.org/animal/hippopotamus/

Ortiz, E. (2021, June 4). Strangest Sports in the World. Stadium Talk. https://www.stadiumtalk.com/s/worlds-strangest-sports-a8bef81c8b8941b3

Pappas, S. (2011, March 17). 10 things you didn't know about dogs. Livescience.Com. https://www.livescience.com/13305-facts-dog-breeds-genetics-pets.html

Parade Magazine. (2021, September 1). 101 Fun Facts You Never Knew, Guaranteed to Totally Blow Your Mind. Parade. https://parade.com/966564/parade/fun-facts/

Peacock Facts. (2020, December 22). Facts.Net. https://facts.net/nature/animals/peacock-facts/

Perimeter Institute. (2018, June 12). 20 illuminating, enlightening, day-brightening facts about light. Inside The Perimeter. https://insidetheperimeter.ca/20-illuminating-enlightening-day-brightening-facts-about-light/

Perritano, J. (2020, December 17). No Chocolate, No Avocado: 10 Foods Dogs Can't Eat. HowStuffWorks. https://animals.howstuffworks.com/pets/no-chocolate-no-avocado-10-foods-dogs-cant-eat.htm

Pettit, S. (2021, June 9). 30 surprising facts about the Netherlands. Expatica. https://www.expatica.com/nl/moving/about/netherlands-facts-108857/

Peshin, A. (2021, April 14). How Much Current Can The Human Body Withstand? Science ABC. https://www.scienceabc.com/humans/how-many-volts-amps-kill-you-human.html#electric-shock-how-much-electricity-will-kill-you

Pit Bull Facts. (2016, November 30). Villalobos Rescue Center. https://www.vrcpitbull.com/pit-bull-facts/

Pizza Planet. (2019, October 8). We Bet You Didn't Know These Incredible Facts About Pizza. https://www.pizzaplanet.com/incredible-facts-about-pizza/

Plants Facts. (2021, March 13). Facts.Net. https://facts.net/nature/plants/

Poe, H. L. (2019, November 15). 10 Things You (Probably) Didn't Know About C.S. Lewis. Publishers Weekly. https://www.publishersweekly.com/pw/by-topic/industry-news/tip-sheet/article/81733-10-things-you-probably-didn-t-know-about-c-s-lewis.html

Poirot, L. (2021, February 24). 50 Weird Laws Around the World. Far & Wide. https://www.farandwide.com/s/weird-laws-world-4961c1ede8d749bf

Pope, S. (2015, July 22). How An 11-Year-Old Boy Invented The Popsicle. NPR. https://choice.npr.org/index.html?origin=https://www.npr.org/sections/thesalt/2015/07/22/425294957/how-an-11-year-old-boy-invented-the-popsicle

Prior, E. (2021, April 27). 17 Fun Facts You Didn't Know About Italy. Flavours Holidays. https://www.flavoursholidays.co.uk/blog/facts-about-italy/

Psychology Facts. (2020, December 22). Facts.Net. https://facts.net/lifestyle/health/psychology-facts/

Puiu, T. (2021, January 29). 17 Amazing Chemistry Facts that will Blow Your Mind. ZME Science. https://www.zmescience.com/science/chemistry/amazing-chemistry-facts/

R. (2021, March 7). 49 Sports Facts – Nr. 26 Is Unbelievable. Only Fun Facts. https://onlyfunfacts.com/fun-facts/sports-facts/

Rafflesia, The World's Largest Bloom. (n.d.). Rafflesia Flower. http://www.rafflesiaflower.com/Rafflesia-Facts.html

Rai Of Light. (2021, May 10). 100 Interesting and Fun Mexico Facts to know | Visit Mexico City. A Rai of Light. https://www.araioflight.com/interesting-fun-mexico-facts/

Ransdell, M. (2021, June 2). 77 fun facts about Denmark you need to know. Wonderful Wanderings. https://wonderfulwanderings.com/denmark-facts/

Robinson, M. (2021, March 17). 10 Interesting Facts About The NFL. The Fact Site. https://www.thefactsite.com/nfl-facts/

Rogers, K. (n.d.). Do Hyenas Really Laugh? Encyclopedia Britannica. https://www.britannica.com/story/do-hyenas-really-laugh

Roos, D. (2020, January 27). How Mexican Traditions Work. HowStuffWorks. https://people.howstuffworks.com/culture-traditions/national-traditions/mexican-tradition4.htm

Rossman, J. (2017, April 3). The Most Extreme Temperatures of the Universe. World Science Festival. https://www.worldsciencefestival.com/infographics/extreme-temperatures-universe-infographic/

S. (2021, January 10). 8 Snakes That Give Live Birth Like Mammals & Why (With Pictures!). Reptile Guide. https://reptile.guide/snakes-that-give-live-birth/

Schlottman, A. (2018, May 17). 150 Interesting Facts About Our Favorite Authors [Infographic]. Books on the Wall. https://booksonthewall.com/blog/10-interesting-facts-10-famous-authors/

Schwaller, J. F. (2010, February). Why did the Aztecs only use wheels for toys and not for transport? Mexicolore. https://www.mexicolore.co.uk/aztecs/ask-experts/why-did-the-aztecs-only-use-wheels-for-toys-and-not-for-transport

SciShow Space. (2014, August 5). How Do Astronauts Do Their Business? [Video]. YouTube. https://www.youtube.com/watch?v=AolkPLOV7Io

Sheldon, J. (2016, April 14). 30 Facts You Didn't Know About Past U.S. Presidents. Goliath. https://www.goliath.com/random/30-facts-you-didnt-know-about-past-u-s-presidents/

Sherlock, B. (2020a, January 2). The Lord Of The Rings: 10 Behind-The-Scenes Facts About The Trilogy To Rule Them All. Screen Rant. https://screenrant.com/the-lord-of-the-rings-behind-the-scenes-facts-trivia-the-hobbit/

Sherlock, B. (2020b, March 28). This Is Sparta!: 10 Behind-The-Scenes Facts About 300. Screen Rant. https://screenrant.com/300-behind-scenes-facts-zack-snyder-gerard-butler-movie/

Simply Chocolate. (n.d.). 8 Fun Facts About Chocolate You'll be Glad to Know. https://www.simplychocolate.com/learn-about-chocolate

SleepyLizard. (2020, November 15). Why a Hass Avocado Seed Does Not Give Us a Hass Avocado Tree [Video]. YouTube. https://www.youtube.com/watch?v=yWAR_DotvZs

Space Facts. (2021, June 8). Saturn Facts - Interesting Facts about Planet Saturn. https://space-facts.com/saturn/

Specktor, B. (2018, August 23). 27 Hilarious (but Totally Real) Names for Groups of Animals. Reader's Digest. https://www.rd.com/list/funny-animal-names-group-by-group/

Sterling, J. (2017, June 28). 5 Things You Didn't Know About Piña Coladas. Food & Wine. https://www.foodandwine.com/news/5-things-you-didnt-know-about-pina-coladas

Strauss, B. (2019, January 10). Spinosaurus - Bigger than T. Rex, and Every Bit as Nasty. ThoughtCo. https://www.thoughtco.com/things-to-know-spinosaurus-1093798

Strauss, B. (2019b, September 26). 10 Facts About the Velociraptor, a World-Famous Dinosaur. ThoughtCo. https://www.thoughtco.com/things-to-know-velociraptor-1093806

Super Bowl Facts - 40 Interesting Facts About Super Bowl. (2017, February 13). Kickass Facts. https://www.kickassfacts.com/40-interesting-super-bowl-facts/

Swatman, R. (2017, March 29). Daredevil female entertainer breaks record stopping fans with her tongue - Guinness World Records Italian Show. Guinness World Records. https://www.guinnessworldrecords.com/news/2017/3/daredevil-female-entertainer-breaks-record-stopping-fans-with-her-tongue-guinne-467200

Swerdloff, A. (2015, June 12). How "Jurassic Park" Nearly Drove the Chilean Sea Bass to Extinction. VICE. https://www.vice.com/en/article/bmpby3/how-jurassic-park-nearly-drove-the-chilean-sea-bass-to-extinction

T. (2021b, March 10). Coyote Facts. Facts.Net. https://facts.net/nature/animals/coyote-facts/

Terminology Coordination. (2021, January 18). Male and Female Animal Names. Terminology Coordination Unit. https://termcoord.eu/2018/02/male-and-female-animal-names/

TG Staff. (2018, April 17). Disney: 25 Secrets About Lilo & Stitch That Are Out Of This World. The Gamer. https://www.thegamer.com/disney-lilo-stitch-facts-secrets/

The Fact File. (2021, July 6). 25 Interesting Facts About Lasers. https://thefactfile.org/laser-facts/

The Planets. (2017, August 14). Jupiter Facts: Interesting Facts about Planet Jupiter. https://th eplanets.org/jupiter/

Thomas, E. (2018, April 18). What Are the Dangers of Scuba Diving? Travel Tips - USA Today. https://traveltips.usatoday.com/dangers-scuba-diving-2492.html

Threadgill's. (2015, July 12). 5 Salad Facts That Will Toss Your Mind. https://www.threadgills .com/tnn/2015/7/12/salad-days-of-summer-week-3

Thrillist. (2021, August 9). The 100 Greatest Memes Ever, Ranked. https://www.thrillist.com /entertainment/nation/best-memes-of-all-time

Top 10 facts about rhinos. (2019, September 13). WWF. https://www.wwf.org.uk/learn/fasci nating-facts/rhinos

Tulip - New World Encyclopedia. (n.d.). New World Encyclopedia. https://www.newworlde ncyclopedia.org/entry/Tulip

Upton, E. (2014, January 31). Were Footballs Ever Really Made of Pigskin? Today I Found Out. https://www.todayifoundout.com/index.php/2014/01/footballs-never-made-pigskin/

USGS Water Science School. (n.d.). The Water in You: Water and the Human Body. Retrieved June 17, 2021, from https://www.usgs.gov/special-topic/water-science-school/science/water -you-water-and-human-body?qt-science_center_objects=0#qt-science_center_objects

Wallenfeldt, J. (n.d.). 6 Interesting Facts About Fidel Castro. Encyclopedia Britannica. https:/ /www.britannica.com/list/6-interesting-facts-about-fidel-castro

Waltner, A. (2019, December 1). 25 Interesting facts about Denmark. Swedish Nomad. https: //www.swedishnomad.com/interesting-facts-about-denmark/

Wanjek, C. (2011, October 10). Top 5 Misconceptions About Columbus. Live- science. https://www.livescience.com/16468-christopher-columbus-myths-flat-earth-disco vered-americas.html

WatchMojo.com. (2018, August 2). Top 10 Actors You Didn't Know Were in Anime Films [Video]. YouTube. https://www.youtube.com/watch?v=9cDdJQrO-Nw

What a Life Tours. (2020, August 17). 10 Little-Known Things About Julius Caesar. https://w ww.whatalifetours.com/top-things-to-do-in-rome-2/

What is Roller Derby? The Rules, Sports Gears, and More. (2021, August 17). Facts.Net. https: //facts.net/lifestyle/sports/

Who Invented Toilet Paper? (n.d.). Toilet Paper History. http://www.toiletpaperhistory.net/invented-toilet-paper/who-invented-toilet-paper/

Why did dogs become domesticated and when did this begin? (2019, July 29). Purely Pets Insurance. https://www.purelypetsinsurance.co.uk/blogs/why-did-dogs-become-domesticated-and-when-did-this-begin/

Why Does G Force Kill You? (2020, October 30). Bill Walters Online. https://billwaltersonline.com/qa/why-does-g-force-kill-you.html

Why Not Cuba. (2020, June 1). 23 Interesting Facts about Cuba. https://whynotcuba.com/cuba-interesting-facts/

Wilde, R. (2019, October 22). The Truth Behind 300: Who Really Held Thermopylae. ThoughtCo. https://www.thoughtco.com/did-300-spartans-really-hold-thermopylae-1221097

Wiley, D. (2020, April 10). 30 Fun Facts About Plants. Better Homes & Gardens. https://www.bhg.com/gardening/yard/garden-care/fun-facts-about-plants/

Willings, A. (2021, April 14). The most famous internet memes of all time. Pocket-Lint. https://www.pocket-lint.com/apps/news/140427-best-stupidest-and-most-famous-internet-memes-around

Worcestershire Sauce. (2014, November 5). Ten Random Facts. http://tenrandomfacts.com/worcestershire-sauce/

World Population Review. (2022). Hardest Working Countries 2022. https://worldpopulationreview.com/country-rankings/hardest-working-countries

WWF. (2019c, September 13). Top 10 facts about rhinos. https://www.wwf.org.uk/learn/fascinating-facts/rhinos

WWF. (2019d, November 19). Top 10 facts about elephants. https://www.wwf.org.uk/learn/fascinating-facts/elephants

Y., S. (2020, November 12). 42 Weird Laws Around The World. Factinate. https://www.factinate.com/things/42-weird-laws/

Y., S. (2020, December 18). Swash-Buckling Facts About Pirates. Factinate. https://www.factinate.com/things/51-interesting-facts-about-pirates/

Yahoo!Entertainment. (2013, April 18). Flavor Flav Explains Why He Wears a Clock as a Necklace. https://www.yahoo.com/entertainment/bp/flavor-flav-explains-why-wears-clock-necklace-155453176.html

Yuko, E. (2020, March 24). 35 Fascinating Facts About the Milky Way. Far & Wide. https://w ww.farandwide.com/s/fascinating-facts-about-space-and-our-galaxy-47728a72e5174374